THE MILLENNIUM
BOOK OF DAYS

THE
Millennium
BOOK OF DAYS

Edith Pavese & Judith Henry

Illustrations from the collections of
THE LIBRARY OF CONGRESS

CROWN PUBLISHERS, INC.
NEW YORK

Published by Crown Publishers, Inc.,
201 East 50th Street, New York, New York 10022.
Member of the Crown Publishing Group.

Random House, Inc. New York, Toronto, London, Sydney, Auckland

CROWN is a trademark of Crown Publishers, Inc.

Manufactured in Hong Kong

Project Concept: Edith Pavese
Design: Judith Henry
Design Assistant: Timothy Jeffs

ISBN 0-517-59872-8

10 9 8 7 6 5 4 3 2

FOREWORD

The Millennium Book of Days is a celebration, in images and commemorative notations, of the remarkable events of the years from 1000 A.D. to 2000 A.D. As the millennium sweeps past in this brief and artful presentation, we note hallmarks of human achievement—from Leif Ericsson's explorations to *Voyager*'s passage beyond the bounds of our solar system. Other events, however, serve as cautionary reminders, as we enter a new millennium, that humankind's path through history has been marred by divisiveness and discord, even as it has been marked by discovery and accomplishment.

The images you find in this book of days are drawn from the unparalleled collections of the Library of Congress, which now number over 107 million items in all media, on all subjects, and from all around the world—including written materials in over 460 languages. The Library of Congress is the world's largest library—an institution that serves as the "memory" of a nation whose own remarkable achievements are traced to the strength derived from creating one country with contributions of people from many countries. It is particularly fitting that we join in this celebration of the momentous year 2000, which also marks the two hundredth anniversary of the Library's founding.

Among the many images representing human curiosity and inventiveness found in this book are depictions of computer components, crucial elements in what has been called the greatest revolution in information-sharing technology since the invention of moveable type. The Library of Congress is actively participating in this revolution, placing its bibliographic data and much other information on-line and embarking on an ambitious program to digitize and make accessible elements of its collections. At the same time, we hold fast to the incomparable wealth and artistry represented in books large and small, scholarly and celebratory. In that spirit, we have been pleased to collaborate with Pavese & Henry Books and Crown Publishers on the creation of this book of days.

JAMES H. BILLINGTON
The Librarian of Congress

1 0 0 0

to

1 1 0 0

J A N U A R Y

1

2

3

4

5

6

7

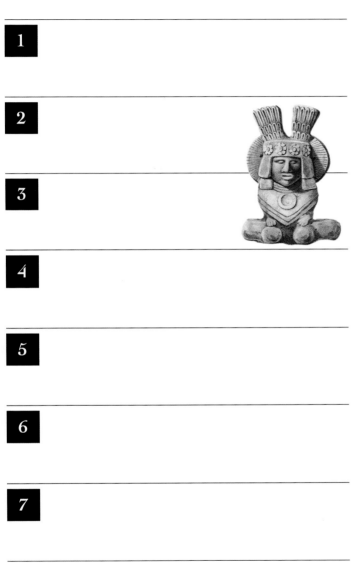

Top left: Birds and foliage grace a Sung dynasty nature painting. Top right: A portion of the Glosas emilianenses, *evidence of the emerging Spanish vernacular language. Bottom: Church of San Marco in Venice, begun in 1063, shows strong influences from the East. This page: A Mexican clay sacrifice figure.*

1000 World population c.265 million. Venice is "Mistress of the sea route to the Holy Land." Roman (Latin) Church dominates western Europe; Greek Orthodox Church dominates eastern Europe. *Beowulf,* the oldest English epic poem, is written down by scribes in Old English. *The Poetic Edda,* 34 epic poems of Norse mythology, is written down in Old Icelandic. **1001** Viking explorer Leif Ericsson reaches North America, an area he calls Vinland, where he finds grapes and wheat growing. Chinese use gunpowder for fireworks. **c.1001** Japanese noblewoman Lady Murasaki no-Shikibu, who is thought to be the first woman novelist, begins the 54-volume *Tale of Genji* about court life. Mahmud, the Turkish Muslim ruler, conquers Pakistan and the Punjab. **1001-50** The Khmer empire is ruled by Suryavarman I. **1010** The Church of the Holy Sepulcher, Jerusalem, is damaged by Al-Hakim, "The Mad Caliph," one of a number of actions that leads to the Crusades. Dia Kossoi, ruler of the Songhoi kingdom in West Africa, converts to Islam.

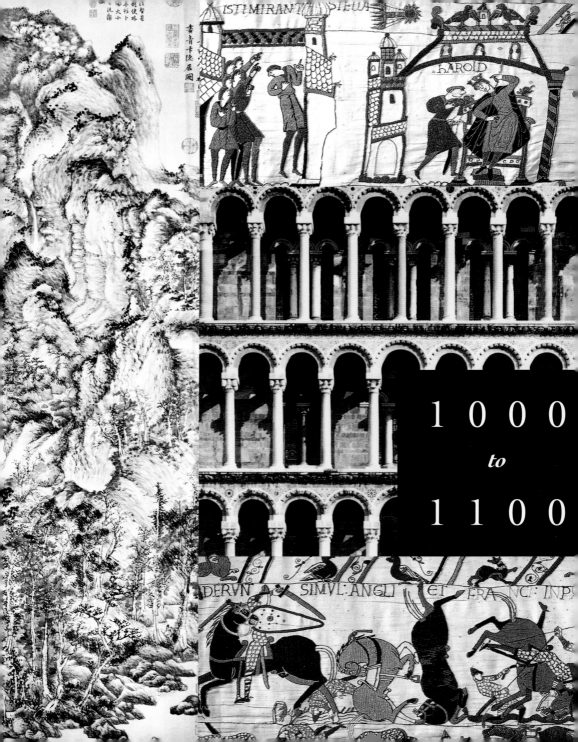

ISTI MIRANT STELLA

HAROLD

DERVN SIMVL: ANGLI ET FRA NCI INP

1 0 0 0

to

1 1 0 0

JANUARY

8

9

10

11

12

13

14

Left: A painting from the Sung dynasty in China. Right top and bottom: Details of the Bayeux Tapestry, *c.1073-83, a 250-foot-long embroidered narrative tapestry depicting William the Conqueror's invasion of England. Right middle: A portion of the richly textured facade of Pisa cathedral, 1063, covered in white marble.*

c.1014-35 Canute forms the Northern Empire of Denmark, Norway, and England; England passes to Edward the Confessor after Canute's death. **1019** *Tao Tsang,* canonical Taoist text, is published. **1019-54** Yaraslov the Wise rules in Russia; he revises and codifies Russian law. **1020** Europe's first recorded merchant guild is founded by traders in Holland. **1024** First known paper currency is issued by the Sung dynasty in China. **c.1030** Ibn Sina (Avicenna) writes an astronomy and physics encyclopedia and *The Canon of Medicine.* Ibn al-Haitam writes *Optical Thesaurus,* the first important work on optics. **1040** Duncan I, king of Scotland, is murdered by Macbeth. **c.1040** A naked Lady Godiva rides a horse through Coventry after her husband promises to reduce taxes if she does this. **1044** Chinese *Wu Chin Tsung Yao* includes a formula for explosives. **c.1045** Chinese develop moveable type made of clay. **c.1050** *Konjaku-Monogatari,* over 700 stories about Japan, China and India, is published. Foot binding becomes popular in China.

1000
to
1100

JANUARY

15

16

17

18

19

20

21

Top: Bas-relief sculpture, portraying scenes from the Old and New Testaments, from the facade of Modena cathedral, begun in 1099. Middle: A verse from the Koran written in Kufic script. Bottom: Detail from the church of St.-Sernin, France, begun c.1080, along the pilgrimage route to Santiago de Compostela in Spain.

1054 The "Final Schism" occurs between the Eastern Orthodox and the Latin churches. Chinese and Japanese astronomers record a supernova. **1057** Macbeth is killed by Duncan's son Malcolm. **1066** William of Normandy defeats the Saxons at the Battle of Hastings and becomes king of England. Construction begins on the Tower of London. **1071** Islamic Turks defeat the Christian Normans at Manzikert, Asia Minor. **c.1071** A two-tined fork is introduced to Venetians by a Greek princess married to the doge. **1072** Kuo Hsi paints his landscape masterpiece *Early Spring*. **1078** Construction begins on the cathedral of Santiago de Compostela, in Spain, over a tomb believed to contain remains of the Apostle James. **1086** Domesday Book survey in British Isles gathers information on land ownership as a basis for taxation. **1092** Walcher of Malvern, after studying an eclipse, tries to calculate the time difference between Italy and England. **1095-99** First Crusade; the Latin Kingdom of Jerusalem is proclaimed by the invading Crusaders.

JANUARY

22

23

24

25

26

27

28

Life in China during the Sung dynasty. By the early twelfth century, the population of Sung China reached about 100 million. Civil officials, who entered their posts through a rigorous examination system, were considered the elite class. Confucian philosophy was dominant. This page: An example of southern Sung dynasty Kuan ware with a crackle finish.

1100 Work begins on the Florence baptistery. **c.1100** Population of Sung Empire in China c.100 million. City of Timbuktu is founded (in present-day Mali). Persian poet, astronomer, and mathematician, Omar Khayyam, is active (d.1123). The crossbow gains in use over the bow and arrow. The magnetic compass first comes into use for navigation. The Khmer Empire in Cambodia reaches its peak. Polyphonic music develops in France. **1104** The Hekla volcano erupts in Iceland, destroying the Viking village of Pjorsardalur. **1113-50** The Khmer Temple of Angkor Wat, noted for extensive, intricate bas-relief sculpture, is constructed. **1115** Pierre Abelard, French theologian and teacher, secretly weds his love Heloise after she gives birth to a son. Florence becomes a republic. University of Bologna is founded. **1115-31** Reign of Stephen II, King of Hungary. **1120** Walcher of Malvern devises measurement of angles in degrees, minutes, and seconds. **1123** Lateran Council forbids marriage of Catholic priests.

1 1 0 0

to

1 2 0 0

J A N U A R Y

29

30

31

1 FEBRUARY

2

3

4

Left: Pisa's bell tower for the cathedral. The tower, constructed in 1174, began "leaning" almost as soon as it was completed, due to the soft subsoil. Right: The Governor's Palace at Uxmal, Mexico, with some 20,000 stone carvings, including those over the main doorway, had already been abandoned by the twelfth century.

1137 Europe's great food market, Les Halles, opens in Paris. **c.1140** Church of St.-Denis, near Paris, is rebuilt by Abbot Sugar in the first example of high Gothic style. **1147** Construction begins on Lisbon cathedral. **1147-49** The failed Second Crusade; many die in Asia Minor. **1148** Byzantine princess, Anna Comnena, probably the first female historian, completes the *Alexiad*, based on her access to imperial archives and knowledge of public affairs. **1150** Paris University is founded. **c.1150** Coal is used at Liège for iron smelting. *The Black Book of Carmarthen*, the first Welsh book, is written. An early form of chess is played in England. **1151** The first fire and plague insurance is issued in Iceland. **1155-90** Frederick I, Barbarossa, proclaims himself the "Holy Roman Emperor" and dominates Italy. **1162** Thomas à Becket is archbishop of Canterbury (he is murdered in the cathedral in 1170). **c.1163** External flying buttresses are first used at the Cathedral of Notre-Dame, Paris. **1166** Cairo citadel is built by Saladin, sultan of Egypt.

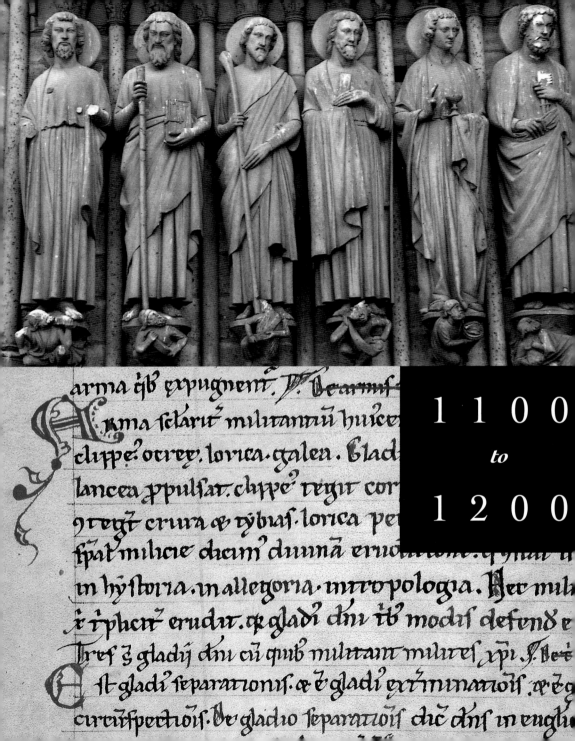

1 1 0 0

to

1 2 0 0

F E B R U A R Y

5

6

7

8

9

10

11

Top: Sculpture from the west facade of the Church of Notre-Dame in Paris, c.1163. Bottom: Esposicio mistica super exod, *a manuscript on vellum, is a fine example of the early Gothic script used in Germany c.1150. This page: Bas-relief stone carving from the temple of Angkor Wat, an architectural masterpiece built 1113-50.*

c.1167 Oxford University is founded. **1170** French poet Chrétien de Troyes writes courtly romance *Le Chevalier à la Charette,* introducing the character Lancelot. **1172** The Venetian Grand Council curbs power of the doges. **1173** First recorded influenza epidemic in Europe. **1174** First recorded public horse races in Europe held at Smithfield, England. Pisa's Bell Tower is completed and begins to "lean" immediately. Cast iron is first produced in Europe. Old London and Avignon bridges are built. **1176** Barbarossa is defeated in Italy. **c.1180** Glass is used for windows in English homes. **1184** Paris paves its first street, a boulevard in front of the Louvre. **c.1185** Kyoto, Japan, is world's largest city with 500,000 inhabitants. Celtic epic *Tristan and Isolde* is written. **1186** Triple coronation in Milan, Italy: Constance of Sicily becomes Queen of the Germans; her husband Henry VI, son of Barbarossa, takes the title of "Caesar"; and Frederick is named King of Burgundy. Astrologers predict great weather calamities, based on conjunction of planets.

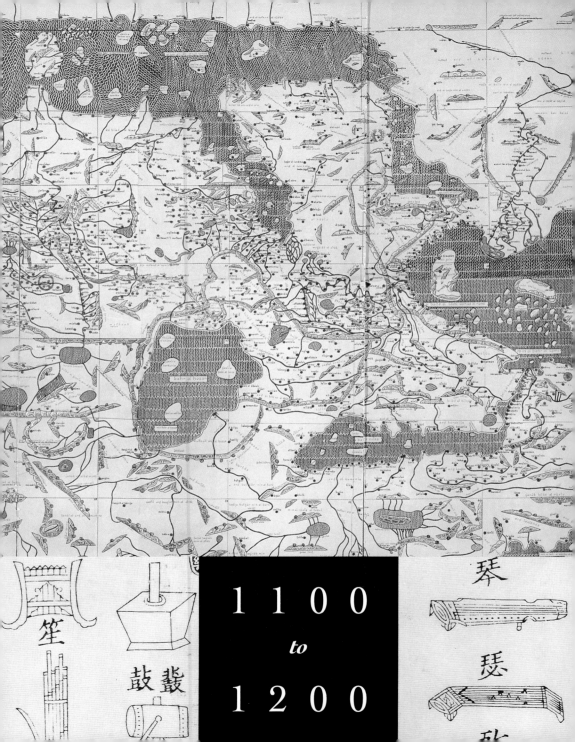

1100
to
1200

FEBRUARY

12

13

14

15

16

Top: An 1154 world map by the Arabian geographer Idrisi, produced over a 15-year period. Here, south is at the top. Bottom: Chinese ceremonial musical instruments from the Shang-shu t'u, Fukien, c.1190. This page: Stained-glass window from Chartres cathedral, c.1194-1220, depicting scenes from the life of Jesus.

1187 United under Saladin, Muslims retake the Latin Kingdom of Jerusalem. **1189-92** The Third Crusade fails to recapture Jerusalem. **1190** *The Guide to the Perplexed* is written by Moses Maimonides, a Cordoban Jew who fled persecution in Spain; the work deeply influences Judaism, Islam, and scholastic Christianity. **c.1190** Tea from China appears in Japan for the first time. **1191** Zen Buddhism is introduced into Japan. **1192** Mohammed of Ghor, sultan of the Afghani principality of Ghanzi, conquers Prithi Raj, the last Hindu ruler of Delhi. The Indian poet Chand Bardi is the first to write in Hindu rather than Sanskrit. **1192-1333** The Kamakura shoguns rule in Japan. **1193** Indigo is used in England for dyeing fabric. Japan licenses prostitution. **1195** Construction begins on Chartres cathedral over an earlier Romanesque church. **1198** Philip II, king of France, is excommunicated by Pope Innocent III for divorcing his wife, Ingeborg of Denmark. **1199** King Richard I of England, called the Lion Hearted, is killed in battle in France.

本草四

1 2 0 0

to

1 3 0 0

F E B R U A R Y

17

18

19

20

21

22

23

Every stage of the manufacture and marketing of salt —from its removal from the sea to its use in cooking by the customer who buys it —is seen in this detail of a painting from the 1249 Sung dynasty Ching shih cheng lei pen ts'ao. *This page: A European knight in armor is shown carrying a martel, c.1220.*

c.1200 Leonardo Fibonacci writes the first western algebra textbook and introduces Arabic (based on Indian) numerals. Mayan city of Chichén Itzá, which had dominated the Yucatan, suffers a severe decline. Manco Capac, first ruler of the Incas, conquers southern Peru and founds Cuzco. Incas develop sophisticated engineering and building skills; they also produce intricate, renowned multicolored woven tapestries. Ife, the Yoruba holy city (in present-day Nigeria), produces naturalistic terracotta heads and bronzes made by the lost-wax technique. Sailing ships begin to use stern rudders. A new strain of rice in China doubles production. Norwegian army troops first use skis. **c.1202** Court jesters first appear in Europe. **1202-04** Fourth Crusade conquers Constantinople. **1203** Construction on church of Mont-Saint-Michel. The Sossos conquer and devastate Ghana kingdom, and enslave the inhabitants of its capital city. **1204** Baldwin I, count of Flanders, is named first emperor of the Latin Empire, which lasts until 1261.

1 2 0 0

to

1 3 0 0

F E B R U A R Y

24

25

26

27

28

29

1 MARCH

Top: Marco Polo arriving at Cathay (China). Middle left: A portrait of Giotto (1267-1336), Florentine painter and architect. Bottom left: Illustration from a volume of English canon law derived from plenary councils held in 1257 and 1268. Right: Facade of Strasbourg cathedral, c.1277. This page: Yuan dynasty porcelain vase with lid.

1206 Temujin is proclaimed Genghis Khan ("Universal Ruler"), beginning the Mongol empire. **1209** Cambridge University is founded. **1211** Construction of Reims cathedral begins on traditional site of the coronation of French kings. **1212** "Children's Crusade" led by religious visionary Stephen of Cloyes; about 30,000 children reach Marseilles and are lured aboard ship by slave dealers and sold in Egypt. Christian victory of Navas de Tolosa over the Moors in Spain. **c.1212** Japanese Buddhist poet-essayist Kamo no Chomei writes *Hojoki*, which contrasts court ceremonies with his hermit existence as a monk. **1213-15** *Heike Monogatari*, a popular prose epic of Japanese clan rivalry, is written down. **1215** King John of England is forced to sign the Magna Carta at Runnymede, limiting royal power. The Fourth Lateran Council asks Jews and Muslims to wear badges to identify themselves. **1218** Denmark adopts the Donneborg, a red flag with a white cross, as its emblem (it is the oldest existing national flag in the world).

les culta erūt. Et diūta captiuitate exercit[us]
istr̄l. et edificabūt ciuitates desertas. ⁊ habi
tabūt in eas. ⁊ plantabūt uineas ⁊ bibēt
uinū eax. Et faciēt ortos ⁊ comedent
fructus eox. Et plantabo eos sup̄ humū s.
⁊ nō euella eos ultra de tra. s. quā dedi
eis. dicit d̄s dc̄rius.

Bdias q̄ interptat̄ ser
uus d̄i ꝓnat in edo. ⁊ sanguiē
teneū; frīs iacob sep emulū: ha
sta primū hospitali.

⟨I⟩n uisio abdie.
Hec dicit d̄s d̄s ad edō.
Auditū audiuim̄
a dn̄o ⁊ legatū ad
ḡs misit. Surgite
⁊ consurgam̄ aduisum
eū in plīū. Ecce paruulū dedi te in
gentib; ⁊ c̄temptibil's tu es ualde. Su
bia cordis. t. extulit te hitantē i cā
suris petre ⁊ exalta te soliū. s. q̄ dic
i corde. s. q̄s detrahet me i tr̄ā; ⁊ ex
altat sicut ut aq̄la elī si iter sidera posu
is nidū: ide detrahā te dc̄lic d̄s. Si fures i
tuisset ad te. si latrones p̄ nocte. quō c̄tic

[right column:]

uit ex eis. Et tū
die pc̄tionis.
os iuda i die p̄
ntificab os. t. in

retributioē. t.
tū. et. bibistis si
os ḡs q̄ iugit. ⁊ b
q̄ n̄ sit. Et ituo
er s̄cōs ⁊ possidē
se possederūt.
⁊ dom̄ ioseph fla
pla. ⁊ succc̄de
eos. ⁊ nō erit rel
locut'; ⁊. Et here
austrū. montē
philistīm. ⁊ p
tra ⁊ regioē sa
possidebūt galaad

MARCH

2

3

4

5

6

7

8

A magnificent illuminated page from the thirteenth-century Biblia Latina, *hand painted on vellum, probably in England. It is a fine example of Gothic script with chapter headings painted in blue with red decoration. This page: The golden seal of King Andrew II of Hungary, which was affixed to a 1221 document.*

1221 Mongols conquer West Turkistan and Afghanistan. **1223** Mongols invade Persia, China, and Russia. **1225** Construction begins on 238-foot-high red sandstone and white marble Outb Minar tower in New Delhi, India. **1227** Genghis Khan dies. **1228** Francis of Assisi is canonized two years after his death. **c.1230** Candles on birthday cakes for children are first seen in Germany. **1233** Pope Gregory IX empowers the Dominican Order to conduct the Inquisition. The Japanese royal family begins to stain its teeth black; this comes to be seen as a sign of beauty. **c.1235** Water-powered mechanical saws first used. **1236** The Mongols, under Batu Khan, take Moscow and Kiev. **c.1240** Fashionable European women begin to sway their hips when walking. **1242** Russian hero (later saint of the Russian Orthodox church) prince Alexander Nevsky defeats Teutonic knights. **1244** Jerusalem falls to the Turks. **c.1250** The motet, a polyphonic form of music, develops. **c.1250-1450** Mayapán replaces Chichén Itzá as the dominant city in the Yucatán.

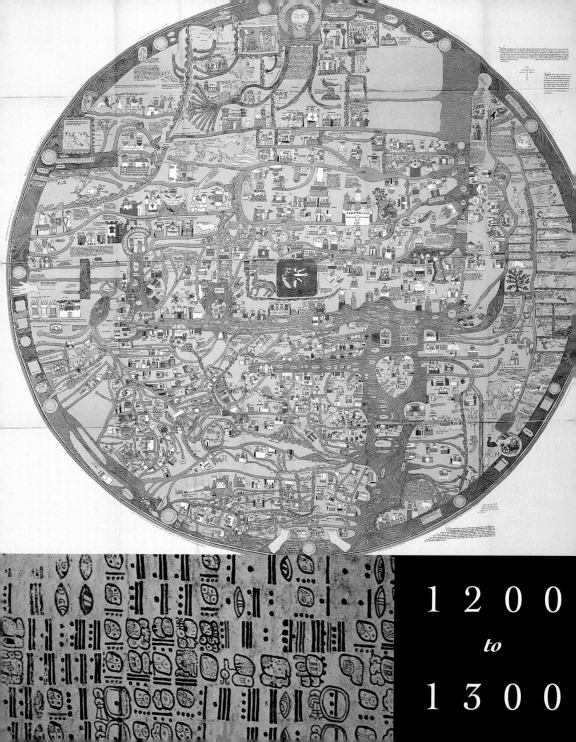

1 2 0 0

to

1 3 0 0

MARCH

9

10

11

12

13

14

15

Top: The 13-foot diameter Ebstorf mappamundi. *The central figure is that of Christ, and the world is arranged more by theological than geographical concerns. Bottom: A detail from the early thirteenth-century* Dresden Codex, *the earliest known Mayan codex, a treatise on astronomy. This page: Tympan of the Gothic church of Mont-Saint-Michel.*

1252 Gold currency is used in Florence and Genoa. **1257** Silk Route from China is opened.**1258** The Mongols capture and sack Baghdad. **1260-94** Reign of Kublai Khan in China. **1264** In *Summa Contra Gentiles* Thomas Aquinas writes arguments to convince non-believers of the truth of Christianity. **1267-68** Roger Bacon writes his three most important works for Pope Clement IV stating his belief in scientific experimentation as the basis for certainty, an idea compatible with religious faith. **1268** An earthquake in southeastern Turkey kills c.60,000 people. **1271-95** Marco Polo travels from Venice to China and serves at the court of Kublai Khan. **1274** The consuls of Montauban, France, forbid wearing of certain furs, silk, and purple garments on the street. **1279-1368** The Mongol dynasty in China founded by Kublai Khan. **1290** Earthquake in northeastern China kills c.100,000. **c.1291** Sugar used as a sweetener is introduced into the west by the returning Crusaders. **1298** The first recorded use of the spinning wheel in Europe.

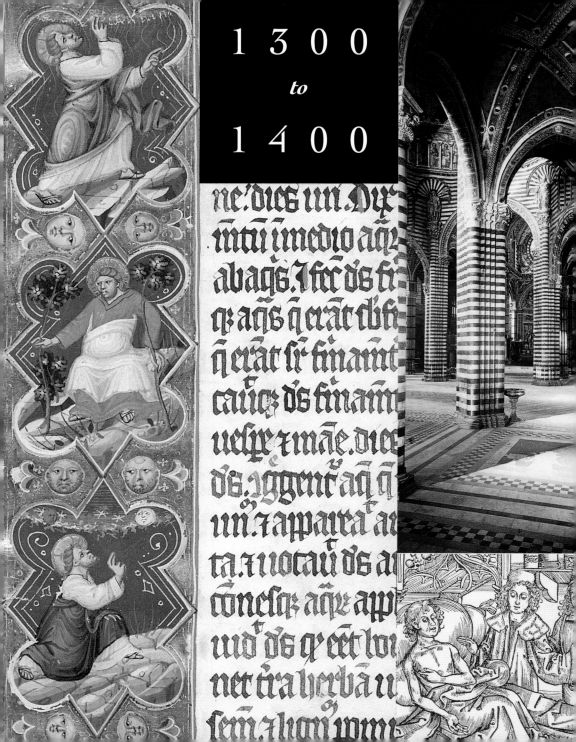

1300 to 1400

MARCH

16

17

18

19

20

21

22

1300 Coal burning in London is forbidden by Edward I, who objects to the dirty air. **c.1300** Eight-acre Emerald Mound near Natchez, Mississippi, is built as ceremonial center. Bowling, with wooden pins and stone balls, is played in Germany. **1304** Arabs use gunpowder as propellant for arrows. **c.1305-06** Giotto paints frescoes in the Arena Chapel, Padua, creating a radical new sense of space in painting. **1306** Jews are arrested and expelled from France. **c.1307** Construction begins on the 900-room Imperial Palace (Forbidden City) in Peking. Dante Alighieri begins *The Divine Comedy.* **1309-77** The "Babylonian Captivity" of the Catholic Church, during which seven popes (from Clement V to Gregory XI) reside at Avignon. **1312-37** Mali empire is at its peak under King Mansa Musa. **1314** Ethiopian (Ge'ez) tale *Kebra Negast* recounts the legend of King Solomon and the Queen of Sheba, traditional founders of Ethiopian (Solomonic) dynasty. Edward II bans football in London, saying it leads to "public disturbances."

Left: A portion of the Nekcsei-Lipocz Bible, *c.1335-40, a Latin Bible on vellum with 146 hand-painted miniatures. Top right : The Romanesque interior of Siena cathedral. Bottom right: An illustration from the* Pestbuch *portrays a victim of the Black Plague. This page: A painting by Giotto shows St. Francis renouncing his possessions.*

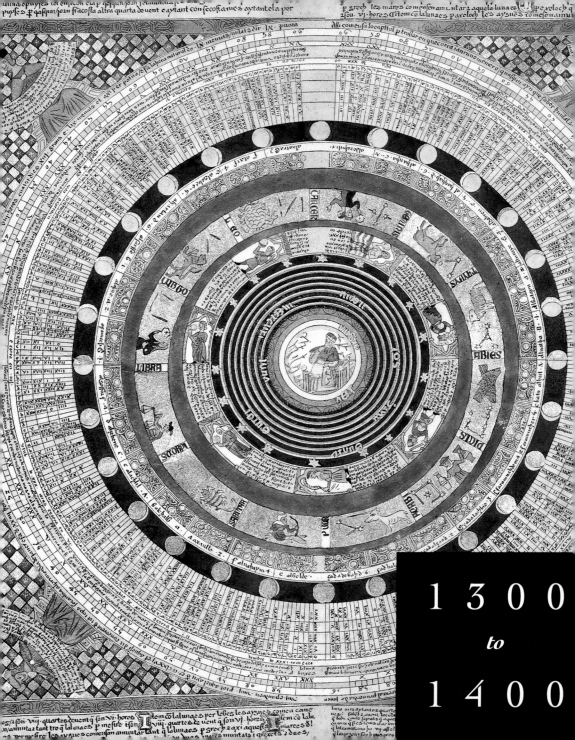

1300
to
1400

MARCH

23

24

25

26

27

28

29

The first leaf of the Catalan Atlas *of 1375, a cartographic masterpiece by Majorcan mapmaker Abraham Cresques, that compiles cosmographical information of the Middle Ages. This page: An illustration of* The Squire's Prologue, *part of Chaucer's* Canterbury Tales, *written c.1387, describing a Christian pilgrimage.*

1314-17 Famine is widespread in England, Ireland, Poland, and the Baltic region. **1321** French guild of minstrels is formed. **1326** The Ottoman Empire is founded when Turks under Osman I defeat the Byzantines in Anatolia. **c.1327** Meister Eckhart, German mystic theologian, dies after being accused of heresy. **1333-37** Earthquakes, floods, drought in China cause c.4 million deaths. **1334-51** Black (Bubonic) Plague kills c.25 million, half of Europe's population. **1337-1453** Hundred Years' War between English and French kings for control of France. **1338-1597** Ashikaga shoguns rule in Japan. **1340** First European paper mill opens at Fabriano, Italy. **1345** Tenochtitlán, the Aztec capital, is founded on Lake Texcoco (near present-day Mexico City). Ottoman Turks first cross into Europe. **1348** Charles IV, the Holy Roman Emperor, founds Charles University in Prague. **1350** The Thai states begin to use the Khmer alphabet. **1353** Giovanni Boccaccio writes *The Decameron (Ten Days of Entertainment).*

1 3 0 0

to

1 4 0 0

MARCH

30

31

1 APRIL

2

3

4

5

Top: Playing cards from a French deck of 1392. Bottom: A view of the Piazza della Signoria, one of the central squares of Florence. The city hall, the Gothic fortress-like Palazzo Vecchio (begun 1298), is at left. This page: A target for a dart game (probably a form of drinking game) used during the Sung dynasty in China.

1365 Tamerlane begins plan to restore the Mongol empire. **1368-1644** The Ming dynasty rules in China. Ming potters are beginning to use an underglaze with a Persian cobalt. **1373** Dutch canals are built with locks. **1375** Dutch fisherman William Benkelsoor develops a method of salting and preserving herring on shipboard. **1378-1417** Rival popes in Rome and Avignon fight for control of the Catholic Church, which begins the "Great Schism." **1379** Ibn-Khaldun writes *Kitab al'Ibar,* a history of Arabs, Berbers, and Muslims in North Africa. **1381** English peasants march on London in an unsuccessful revolt following a 1380 poll tax. **1382** The Vulgate Bible is translated into English. The Burji dynasty begins in Egypt. **c.1387** Poland absorbs Galicia. Geoffrey Chaucer writes *The Canterbury Tales.* **1388** England's first Sanitary Act is passed. **1390** Japanese narrative scrolls illustrated with printed pictures first appear. **1397** The Ottomans sack Constantinople. **1398-99** Muslims rule from Mesopotamia to Afghanistan.

APRIL

6

7

8

9

10

11

12

1400 India's population c.100 million. **c.1402** Malacca is founded as a center of trade in southeast Asia. **1405** Chinese admiral Cheng Ho begins his extensive diplomatic and trade expeditions to southeast Asia, India, Ceylon, Arabia, Egypt, and East Africa with a fleet of 63 junks carrying approximately 28,000 men. **1407** Bethlem Royal Hospital, England, popularly known as Bedlam, becomes an insane asylum, giving rise to use of the word "bedlam." **1411-13** Donatello, the greatest sculptor of this period, works on his statue of *St. Mark* for Or San Michele in Florence. **1413** The nine-story Porcelain Pagoda is commissioned by Emperor Yung Lo for Nanking, China. **1414-18** The "Great Schism" is ended by the Council of Constance, which gives the Roman Pope control of the Catholic Church. **1414-76** The Medicis of Florence are bankers to the Popes. **c.1415** Because of the regular trade between Europe and the East, lavish Oriental designs for fashion and decoration begin to be seen throughout Europe.

Top: A detail from the 1455 Gutenberg Bible, the first book to be printed in Europe with moveable type. The Bible has 1,282 pages and was printed on sheepskin with type invented by Johann Gutenberg. Bottom: From the 1483 Concilium zu Constanz *(Council of Constance). This page: The San Severino medallion, picturing an Italian* condottiere.

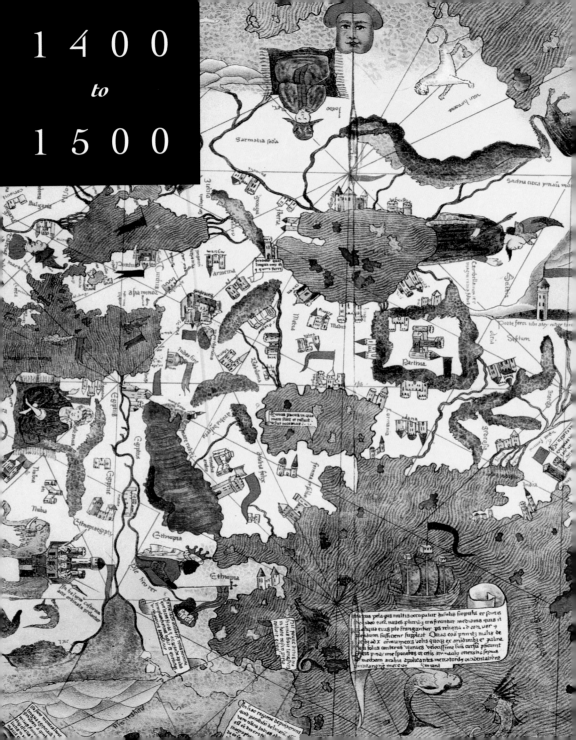

APRIL

13

14

15

16

17

18

19

A 1457 detailed world map by Paolo Toscanelli, a noted Florentine cosmographer and physician. Some years after this map was completed, Toscanelli proposed a westward route from Europe to the East to Christopher Columbus. This page: A fanciful dragon is shown with concealed weapons, from De Re Militari, *1472.*

1416 *Al-Quamus,* an Arabic dictionary, is compiled by Al-Firuzabadi. Religious reformer Jan Hus is burned at the stake for heresy. Christine de Pisan writes *Le Livre de trois vertus* defending rights of women to a full education, and, as writers, to be regarded on equal terms with male authors. Venice is at war with Ottomans over Turkish activity in Aegean Sea; Turkish fleet is destroyed at Gallipoli and peace ensues. **1418** Vietnamese resistance to Chinese occupation is organized by Le Loi, a peasant. **c.1425-30** Donatello completes bronze *David.* **1428** Joan of Arc leads the French against the English (she is burned at the stake as a witch in 1431). **1428-1519** The Aztecs rule in Mexico. **c.1431** After raids by the Thai, Angkor falls. Portuguese sailor Gonzalo Cabral lands in the Azores. **1432** *The Ghent Altarpiece* completed; probably by both Jan and Hubert van Eyck. **c.1437** Counterpoint in music develops. **1438** The Incas rule in Peru. **c.1440** Period of disintegration of Mayan empire. **1442** First tarot cards are used in Ferrara.

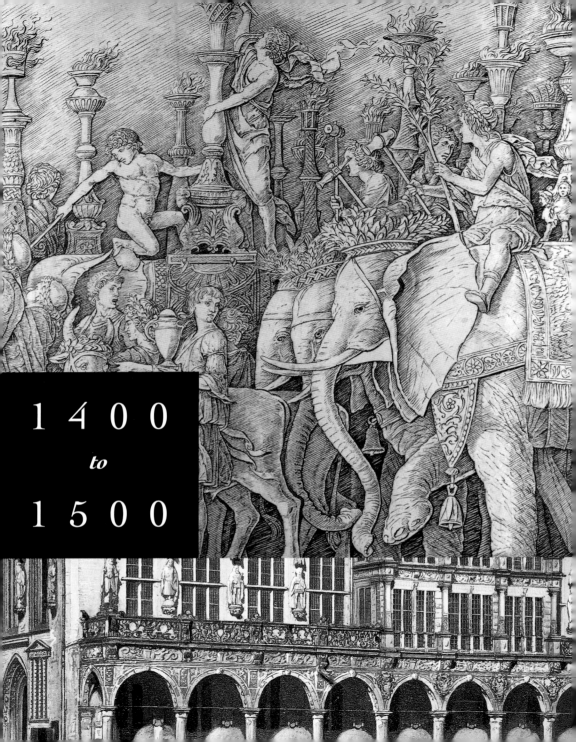

1 4 0 0
to
1 5 0 0

A P R I L

20

21

22

23

24

25

Top: A detail of The Triumph of Caesar, *1484-92, by Andrea Mantegna, one of the most important painters of the early Renaissance period. He is known for his original sense of perspective and love of antiquity. Bottom: The Gothic Town Hall of Bremen, Germany, 1405-09. This page: From* Dialogus Creaturarum, *1480.*

1445 Plague strikes England. Portuguese explorer Dinis Diaz sails around Cape Verde. **1446-50** Johann Gutenberg invents moveable type for printing. (Europeans are unaware of earlier use of moveable type in the Far East.) **1447** Pope Nicholas V founds the Vatican Library. **1450** University of Barcelona is founded. The modern keyboard for the organ is developed. Lorenzo Ghiberti completes *The Gates of Paradise* doors for the Florence baptistery. **1453** The Byzantine empire falls as Turks conquer Constantinople after a 50-day siege. Moscow is now considered the center of the Eastern Orthodox Church. **1455-85** Wars of the Roses between rival noble factions in England. **c.1460** Dentistry is practiced by barbers. **1462-1505** Ivan the Great, the first czar, rules Russia. **1464** Louis XI of France establishes French Royal Mail. **1465** The Zeneta Berbers control Fez, ending the Moroccan Marinid dynasty (dating from c.1200). **1470** Pliny's *Historia naturalis* is published. **1471** Pliny sets up the first European observatory.

1400
to
1500

CIVITAS VENECIARV

A P R I L

26

27

28

29

30

1 MAY

2

Top left: Gold-leafed initial from the Washington Haggadah, *1478.*
Top right: Fasciculus medicinae, *1495, by Johannes de Ketham, the*
first medical treatise with realistic illustrations. Bottom: Venice depicted
by Bernhard von Breydenbach in Journey to the Holy Land, *1486.*
This page: From John Mandeville's Itinerarium, *Augsburg, 1481.*

c.1471 Regiomontanus (Johann Müller) reports his observations of a comet (which is later called Halley's Comet) beginning modern astronomy of comets. John Hartlieb writes the first complete book of palm-reading. **1474** *Terminorum Musicae Diffinitorum,* the first music dictionary, is published in Naples. **1477** Edward IV of England bans cricket because it interferes with the compulsory practice of archery, on which the army relies. **1478** Bartolomeo Sacchi publishes the first printed cookbook, *Concerning Honest Pleasure and Well-Being.* **1478-92** Lorenzo de' Medici (the Magnificent) rules in Florence. **1479-1504** Ferdinand and Isabella rule as king and queen of Spain. **1480** Ivan III becomes czar of Russia. **1482** Portugal establishes settlements on the Gold Coast of Africa. **1483** Edward V ascends the throne of England at age 12. **1484** Sandro Botticelli paints *The Birth of Venus.* **1485** Ivan III rebuilds the Kremlin. **1487** The Incas conquer the kingdom of Quito; the empire extends from northern Equador into Chile and Bolivia.

1 4 0 0

to

1 5 0 0

MAY

3

4

5

6

7

8

9

1490 Italic type is first used in Venice by Aldo Manuzio (Aldus Manutius). c.1490 The toothbrush is invented in China. 1492 Christopher Columbus lands in the Caribbean islands. Spain conquers the Moorish capital of Granada. Jews are expelled from Spain. 1493 Columbus returns to Spain from the New World and introduces tobacco to Europeans. 1494 The Treaty of Tordesillas establishes areas of control by Portugal and Spain in the New World, Africa, and the Far East. 1495 Maximilian I, the Holy Roman Emperor, establishes a Court of Justice to mediate between warring princes and to act as the highest court of appeals for common citizens. 1497 Sailing from Bristol, England, John Cabot reaches and explores the coast of North America. Vasco da Gama sails around the Cape of Good Hope and, in 1498, discovers a sea route to India. Leonardo da Vinci paints his masterpiece *The Last Supper*. 1499 African slave trade begins in Lisbon as a result of the exploration of the west coast of Africa by the Portuguese.

Top left: A 1494 woodcut of Columbus' ships and islands of the Bahamas. Top right: From Buch de Natur, *1481. Bottom left: From* Apocalypsis Sancti Johannis *(Revelation of St. John), c.1470. Bottom right: From* Dialogus Creaturarum, *1480, by Gerard Leeu, with a fable of the sun and moon. This page: From a 1479 edition of* Aesop's Fables.

quarta pars per Americū Vesputiū (vt in sequent
bus audietur) inuenta est / quā non video cur quis
iure vetet ab Americo inuentore sagacis ingenij v
Ameri: ro Amerigen quasi Americi terrā / siue American
ca dicendā: cū & Europa & Asia a mulieribus sua sor
tita sint nomina. Eius situ & gentis mores ex bis b
nis. Americi nauigationibus quæ sequun̄ liquide

MAY

10

11

12

13

14

15

16

Top: The word "America" first appears in the 1517 Introduction to Cosmography *by Martin Waldseemüller, who thought that Amerigo Vespucci was the first European to reach the New World and named it in his honor. Bottom: St. Augustine, Florida, in a 1589 map. This page: From Strabo's* De situ orbis, *a 1510 geographical encyclopedia.*

1500 World population c.400 million. Vincente Pinzon, the commander of Columbus' ship *Nina*, discovers the mouth of the Amazon river. **c.1500** Glass is used instead of oiled paper in French windows. **1501** Amerigo Vespucci explores the east coast of South America. Michelangelo begins the statue of *David*. Shah of Persia defeats the Sunni Turkoman leader of the Ak Koyunlu dynasty (rulers of eastern Anatolia since 1378). **c.1503-06** Leonardo da Vinci paints *Mona Lisa*. **1504** Venice proposes construction of a Suez Canal to the sultan of Turkey. **1508-12** Michelangelo paints the Sistine Chapel ceiling at the Vatican. **1509** Peter Henlein of Nuremberg makes the first portable timepiece. Erasmus of Rotterdam publishes *In Praise of Folly*. **1511** English King Henry VIII bans lawn bowling because it leads to "vicious gambling." **1513** Machiavelli's *The Prince* is published. Ponce de Leon lands in Florida, possibly the first Spaniard to step onto the North American continent. Balboa is the first European to see the Pacific Ocean.

1500
to
1600

M A Y

17

18

19

20

21

22

23

Top: In the 1520s, Albrecht Dürer published advanced theories of perspective. Left: The 1531 Huejotzingo Codex, part of a legal action by Hernando Cortes against the high court of Spain in Mexico. Right: From a 1524 Book of Hours. This page: A map from Macrobius' In somnium scipionis exposito.

c.1514 Pineapples from the Americas first appear in Europe. **1516** The ghetto is established in Venice. **1517** Ottoman conquest of Egypt. Martin Luther posts his 95 theses, which include denouncing the sale of indulgences, on the church door in Wittenberg, beginning Reformation in Germany. **1519** Hernando Cortes enters the Aztec capital of Tenochtitlán and takes Emperor Montezuma II as a hostage. Aztec princess Malintzin is offered to the conquistadors in exchange for peace; she becomes Cortes' mistress and guide, translating Mayan and Nahuatl languages. **1519-22** Ferdinand Magellan circumnavigates the globe. **1520** Luther is excommunicated by Pope Leo X. Chocolate from the New World is introduced into Spain. **1523-66** Reign of Suleiman I, the Magnificent, over the Ottoman empire. **1524** Giovanni Verrazano explores the east coast of North America from Florida to Nova Scotia. **1525** Incan ruler Huayna Capac dies; his sons quarrel over succession, leaving the Incas unprepared to repel the Spanish invaders.

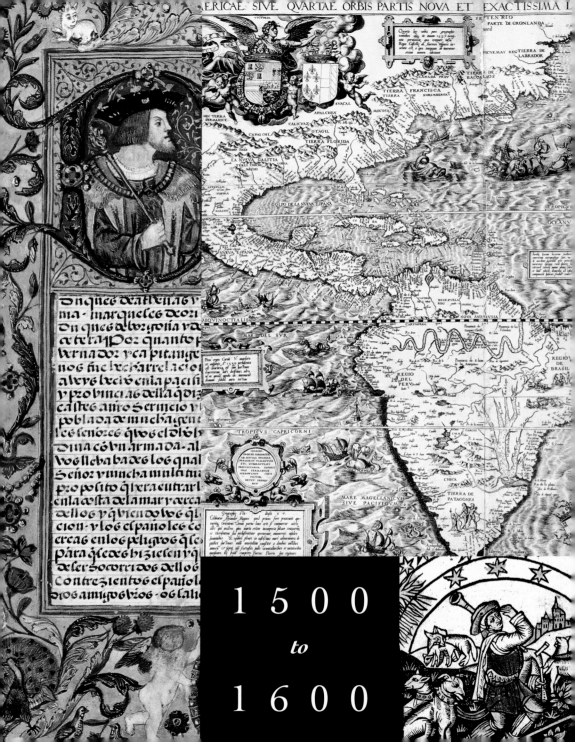

1 5 0 0

to

1 6 0 0

M A Y

24

25

26

27

28

29

30

Left: A 1525 Royal Cedula in which King Charles I grants Cortes a coat of arms in honor of his explorations for Spain. Top right: Diego Gutierrez's 1562 map of the Americas. Bottom right: From the 1516 Shepherd's Calendar, which, like a farmer's almanac, offers practical advice for everyday activities. This page: From a 1566 Roman law book.

1526-30 Mogul emperor Babar extends his rule in India. **1531** The Antwerp Bourse opens, probably first international stock exchange. **1533** Sugar plantations in Brazil. The first book of madrigals is printed in Rome. **1533-84** Reign of Ivan the Terrible in Russia. **1535** Francisco Pizarro founds Lima, Peru, as the capital of the Portuguese viceroyalty. **1536** Anne Boleyn, second wife of Henry VIII, is beheaded after being found guilty of adultery and incest. **1542** The rupee is introduced as monetary unit in India. **1543** *De revolutionibus orbium coelestium* by Nicholas Copernicus, outlining his theory that planets rotating on their own axes revolve around a stationary sun, is published. *De fabrica corporis humani*, the first modern human anatomy treatise, by Andreas Vesalius, is published. **c.1545** Spanish influence on European fashion. **1546** Martin Luther dies. Italian physician Girolamo Fracastoro develops a contagion theory of disease. Silver mining is established at Potosi, Peru. *De re metallica* on mining, by Georgius Agricola is published.

1 5 0 0

to

1 6 0 0

MAY

31

1 JUNE

2

3

4

5

6

Left: The extraordinary wooden Byzantine Cathedral of St. Basil, Moscow, 1554-60, built during the reign of Ivan the Terrible. Top right: A detail from a late sixteenth-century portolan atlas. Bottom right: A 1587 engraving of a musketeer by Dutch artist Jacob de-Gheyn. This page: A Japanese coin of c.1591.

c.1550 Groundhog Day begins as a German legend in which a badger forecasts spring by seeing his shadow. Candles are used in Europe for indoor lighting. Billiards are played in Italy. **1554** São Paulo, Brazil, is founded by Jesuit missionaries. **1555** French astrologer and physician called Nostradamus publishes *Centuries,* rhymed prophesies of mankind's future. **1556-1605** Mogul emperor Akbar the Great rules in India. **1557** Portuguese are established at Macao and trade regularly with China (making Macao oldest permanent European settlement in Asia). **1563** English Statute of Apprentices mandates seven years of apprenticeship to practice a trade. **1564** Roman Catholic Church publishes *Index expergatorius,* a list of books forbidden to Catholics. Giorgio Vasari's *Lives of the Artists* is published. Graphite is first used for pencils. **c.1565** Modern form of ice cream is made in Florence (flavored ice was reported by Marco Polo on his return from China). **1568** Gerardus Mercator develops cylindrical map projections.

1 5 0 0

to

1 6 0 0

J U N E

7

8

9

10

11

12

13

Left: From Thomas Hariot's 1590 "A briefe and true report of the new found land of Virginia." Top right: From Diego Duran's Historia Antigua de la Nueva España, 1581. Bottom right: 1544 Agnese world map with Magellan's 1519-21 circumnavigation route. This page: Taino Indians pan for gold, from La Historia General de las Indias, 1535.

1569 The government of Spain declares bankruptcy. **1570** Japan opens ports to foreign ships, ending its period of isolation. **1571** Battle of Lepanto; Holy League defeats Ottoman fleet. Spanish forces found the city of Manila after conquest of its Muslim settlement. **1572** Rafael Bombelli uses imaginary numbers in his book *Algebra*. Tycho Brahe observes a supernova and produces first modern star catalog, *De nova stella*, stating that the universe is dynamic and not a fixed system. **1573** Construction begins on Mexico City cathedral. **1575** Trade treaty is signed by Portuguese and Monomotapa empire (present-day Zimbabwe). Painter El Greco begins to work in Spain. **1578** Work begins on Pont Neuf in Paris, the first bridge over the Seine. **1579** Francis Drake claims California for England. **1580** Montaigne's *Essays*, condemning superstition, are published. **1582** Pope Gregory XIII introduces New Style (Gregorian) Calendar; the calendar no longer uses April 1 as New Year's Day and it is known as "fool's holiday" for those who resist the change.

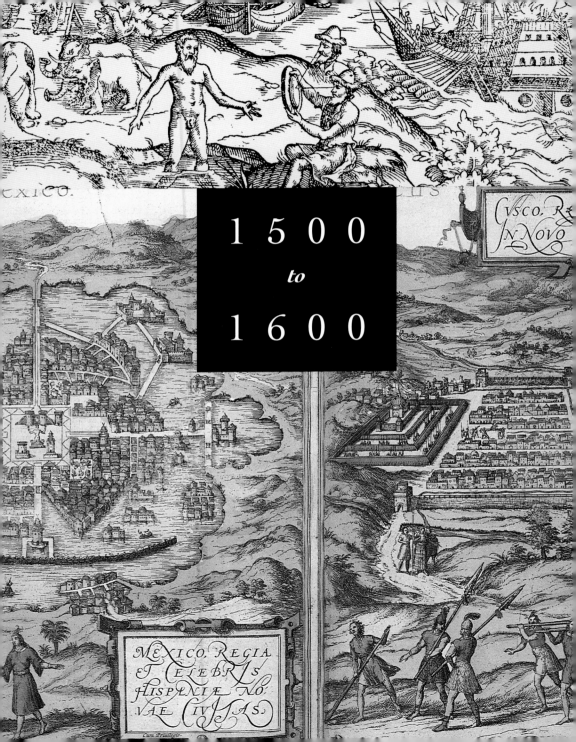

1 5 0 0

to

1 6 0 0

CVSCO. R_X IN NOVO

MEXICO. REGIA ET CELEBRIS HISPANIÆ NOVÆ CIVITAS.

JUNE

14

15

16

17

18

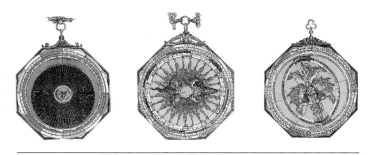

Top: Woodcut from Opticae thesaurus, *1572, showing the refractive properties of water. Bottom: Bird's-eye views of Mexico City and Cuzco, Peru, when the Spanish arrived in the New World, published in 1564. This page: Volvelles (moveable circles) for astronomical calculations, from Petrus Apianus'* Astronomicum Caesareum, *1540.*

1583 Under Hideyoshi construction begins on Osaka Castle, Japan. The first known life insurance policy is issued in England on the life of William Gibbons. **c.1585** Kabuki theater develops in Japan. The decimal point comes into general use in mathematics. **1588** The Spanish Armada is defeated by the English fleet. **1590** Zacharias Janssen, a Dutch eyeglass maker, invents the compound microscope. **1592** Japanese regent-dictator Toyotomi Hideyoshi invades Korea in the first of many failed attempts to establish a military base for the conquest of China. **1594** The House of Bourbon is established in France. **1596** Johannes Kepler's *Mysterium cosmographicum (Mysteries of the Cosmos)*, astronomy text, is published. A type of flush toilet is designed by the English courtier John Harrington. **1597** Dom Joao Dharmapala, a Christian king in Ceylon, dies and leaves his Singhalese kingdom to the Portuguese. **1598** William Shakespeare writes the comedy *Much Ado About Nothing*. **1598-1605** Reign of Boris Godunov, czar of Russia.

1 6 0 0
to
1 7 0 0

JUNE

19

20

21

22

23

24

25

Top left: Nagoya Castle, completed 1611, Nagoya, Japan. Top right: From Johannes Hevelius' Selenographia, 1647. *Bottom: One of the world's fabled buildings, the Taj Mahal in Agra, India, with the reflective pool that enhances its magnificence. The building was constructed by Shah Jahan, a Muslim ruler of India, as a mausoleum for his wife.*

1600 World population c.545 million. English East India Company is founded. English physicist William Gilbert publishes a treatise on electricity (a word he coined) and magnetism. **c.1600** Refracting telescope is developed by Dutch opticians. **1602** Dutch East India Company founded. **1602-27** War between Turkey and Persia. **c.1602** Shakespeare writes *Hamlet.* **1603-1867** Tokugawa shoguns rule in Japan with Edo as its capital. **1604-47** Lope de Vega's 25-volume *Comedias* is published. **1605** Part I of Cervantes' *Don Quixote* is published. **1606** First recorded European landing on Australia is made by Dutch ship *Duyfken.* Galileo invents the proportional compass. **1607** First permanent English colony on American mainland established at Jamestown, Virginia. **1608** First permanent French colony in North America established at Quebec. **1609** Johannes Kepler publishes his laws of planetary motion. Dutch East India Company introduces tea from China to Europe. Morisco descendants of Muslims are expelled from Spain.

1600
to
1700

JUNE

26

27

Deus mortuorum

28

29

30

1 JULY

2

Top: On a 1618 map by Diego Cisneros, Mexico City is still partly surrounded by Lake Tenochtitlán. Bottom left: A playing card factory. Bottom right: Chinese Buddhist Diamond Sutra, 1629. This page: From the 1622 Descriptio Indiae Occidentalis, *an atlas by Antonio de Herrera y Tordesillas, the first historian of the Spanish colonies in America.*

1609-16 Blue Mosque in Constantinople is built. **1610** Galileo announces results of the first telescopic observations of celestial phenomena. **1611** The King James version of the Bible is published in England. **1612** Ferdinand II becomes king of Hungary and Bohemia. **1613** Romanov dynasty begins in Russia. Hungary is invaded by Turks. The Globe Theatre, London, is destroyed by fire. **1616** William Shakespeare dies. **1616-20** Tatars invade China. **1620** The *Mayflower* lands at Plymouth Rock (present-day Massachusetts), bringing the first Pilgrim settlers to North America. **1621** Swedish King Gustav II Adolf invades Polish Livonia, thereby completing Swedish control of Baltic Sea. **1623** Velazquez becomes court painter to Philip IV of Spain. **1628** William Harvey is the first to describe the circulation of blood in humans. **1629** Kabuki theater performances are temporarily banned until boys replace female performers. **1630** Tirso de Molina first uses the stock character Don Juan in literature in *El Burlador de Sevilla.*

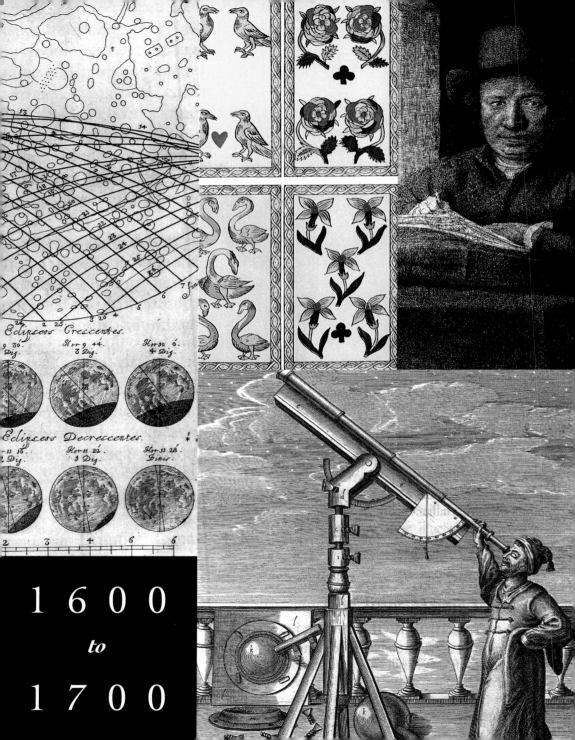

Eclipseos Crescentes.

9 30.   Hor 9 44.   Hor 30 6.
3 Dig.   3 Dig.   4 Dig.

Eclipseos Decrescentes.

Hor 22.   Hor 22 22.   Hor 33 28.
Dig.   3 Dig.   Finis.

2   3   4   5   6

1 6 0 0

to

1 7 0 0

J U L Y

3

4

5

6

7

8

9

Left: Eclipsis Luna *from astronomer Johannes Hevelius'* Selenographia, *1647, an atlas of the moon's surface. Top middle: French playing cards, c.1650, showing flowers, birds, and quadrupeds. Top right: Drawing at* the Window, *1648, a self-portrait by Rembrandt Van Rijn. Bottom: A* Man Observing the Moon *from* Selenographia.

1632 Galileo's *Dialog of Two Major World Systems* is published. **1633** The Inquisition forces Galileo to recant his belief in Copernican theory. **1635** Japan begins a long period of isolation, allowing only the Dutch to continue to trade with them. Académie Française is founded, setting standards of French grammar. **1636** Harvard College is founded. **1637** René Descartes' treatise on analytic geometry is published. **1638** The log cabin is introduced to America by Swedish settlers in Pennsylvania. **1640** Portugal gains independence from Spain. **1642** Rembrandt paints *The Night Watch (The Company of Captain Frans Banning Cocq)*. **1643** The mercury barometer is invented by Evangelista Torricelli. **1643-1715** Louis XIV, the Sun King, rules in France by "divine right." **1644** The Manchus conquer China and begin the Ch'ing dynasty; Peking becomes the capital. **1644-94** Matsuo Basho is considered the greatest of Japanese haiku poets. **1647** Sivaji, Hindu rebel against dominant Muslim Mogul empire, begins conquests in India.

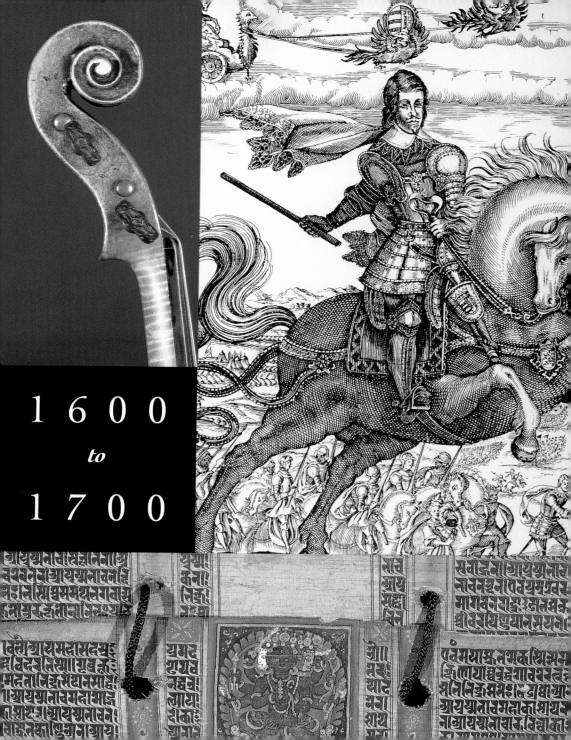

1 6 0 0

to

1 7 0 0

J U L Y

10

11

12

13

14

15

16

Top left: The scroll of the Kreisler Guarnerius violin. Top right: An allegorical print of Ferdinand III (1608-57), king of Hungary and Bohemia, shows his victories in war and various symbols of his life and reign. Bottom: A Nepalese painted wooden book cover and a manuscript leaf with a Buddhist text in Sanskrit.

1648 End of the Thirty Years' War. Margaret Jones is the first person executed as a witch in America for possessing a "malignant touch" that caused illness or deafness. **c.1650** Young girls in Europe dress in long gowns with lace collars. **1651** Giovanni Battista Riccioli creates a map of the moon with many names of lunar features that are still used. **1657** Gianlorenzo Bernini designs the Colonnade for St. Peter's, Rome. **1660** Actresses first appear on the English stage. **1661** English capture West African Dutch trading fort at the mouth of the Gambia River; named Fort James, it is the first permanent British settlement in Africa. **1664** Dutch surrender New Amsterdam to the English and its name is changed to New York. **1664-65** More than 70,000 (of c.460,000) die of Bubonic Plague in London. **1666** The Great Fire of London. **1667** End of the Thirteen Years' War fought between Russia and Poland over Ukraine. **1670** Minute hands for clocks developed by British clockmaker William Clement (before this, only hour hands were used).

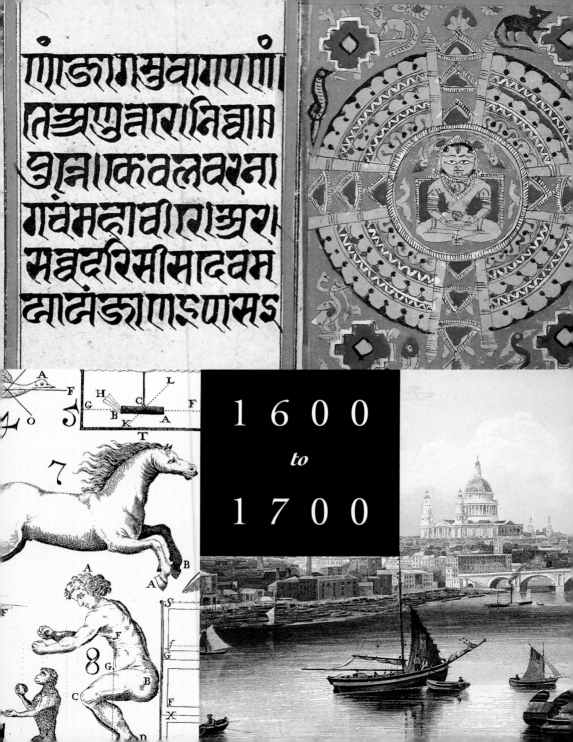

1 6 0 0
to
1 7 0 0

J U L Y

17

18

19

20

21

22

23

Top: A text in Prakrit from an Indian Kalpa Sutra. Bottom left: From Giovanni Borelli's 1685 De motu animalium, *a treatise on motion, here illustrating the center of gravity in moving animals. Bottom right: St. Paul's Cathedral in London, 1675-1709, designed in classical style by architect Sir Christopher Wren.*

1672 The first concert for which an admission fee is charged is given by John Banister, an English violinist, in London. **1676** Danish astronomer Olaus Roemer postulates a finite velocity for light. **1677-1681** Following war with Russia, Treaty of Radzin forces Turks to cede most of Ukraine and give Cossacks trading rights on the Black Sea. **1680** Christiaan Huygens develops a gunpowder-fueled internal combustion engine. **1682** Halley first observes the comet that later bears his name and predicts future appearances. **1683** Chinese Ch'ing dynasty emperor Sheng Tsu conquers Taiwan from rebel members of the Ming dynasty. **1687** Isaac Newton states his principle of universal gravitation. Turks revolt against Mohammed IV, Ottoman sultan, who is deposed and succeeded by his brother Suleiman II. **1689** Peter the Great becomes czar of Russia; he forbids the traditional wearing of beards. William III and Mary II begin rule in England. **1690** Pressure cooker, called "steam digester," is invented by French physicist Denis Papin.

1700 to 1800

J U L Y

24

25

26

27

28

29

30

Left: A 1702 Dutch Bible illustrated by Romeyn de Hooghe. Top right: Frontispiece of De statica medicina *by Santorio Santorio showing his weighing chair in which he could measure every bodily change during his work day. Bottom right: Mongolian Buddhist Sutra in ink, gouache, and brocaded silk on paper. This page: A 1704 coin from Strasbourg.*

1700 c.1 million Native Americans live in area of present-day U.S. and Canada. Boston is the largest city in the colonies with population of c.7,000. **1701** Holy Roman Empire, Great Britain, and the Netherlands sign Treaty of the Hague. Captain William Kidd is hanged for piracy. **1702** *The Daily Courant,* the first daily newspaper, is published in London. **1703** Earthquake and fire at Edo kill c.200,000. **1704** Isaac Newton publishes *Opticks* on his experiments with the reflection, refraction, diffraction, and spectra of light. **1705** Edmund Halley notes the similarities in comets of 1531, 1607, 1682; he predicts a return in 1758. The Husain dynasty of Tunis is established by Spanish Muslims expelled from Spain; Turkish authority is overthrown. **1707** Mt. Fuji in Japan erupts (it has not erupted since). The United Kingdom of Great Britain—England, Wales, and Scotland—is formed. **1710** The population of Europeans living in North America is c.300,000. **1711** The first horse races at Ascot, England, take place.

JULY

31

1 AUGUST

2

3

4

5

6

Top: From Matthew Seutter's 1745 Atlas Novus. *Bottom left: A 1724 engraving published in Paris shows young Iroquois being taught to recite the laws of the Five Nations Confederacy using a beaded belt as an aid to memory. Bottom right:* A New Voyage to Carolina,*1709, by John Lawson, Gentleman Surveyor General of North Carolina.*

1712 Alexander Pope's *Rape of the Lock* is published. **1713** Peace of Utrecht ends the War of Spanish Succession. **1714** Public education begins in Russia. Gabriel Daniel Fahrenheit develops a mercury thermometer with a new system of calibration. Ahmed Bey rules Tripoli; begins the Caramanli dynasty (until 1835). **1714-27** Reign of George I in England. **1716** The *K'ang Hsi* dictionary of some 40,000 Chinese characters is published. **1716-45** Yoshimune, a Tokugawa shogun, reigns in Japan. **1718** The Spanish found San Antonio as a Franciscan mission on the site of a Native American village. **1720** Chinese emperor K'ang Hsi drives Dzungars out of Tibet, destroying the last remnants of Mongol influence there. **1721** Russian Orthodox Church comes under the authority of the state. Johann Sebastian Bach composes the *Brandenburg Concertos.* **1723** First commercial valentines appear. Christianity is banned in China. **1724** Academy of Sciences at St. Petersburg, Russia, is founded by Peter the Great.

1700
to
1800

AUGUST

7

8

9

10

11

12

13

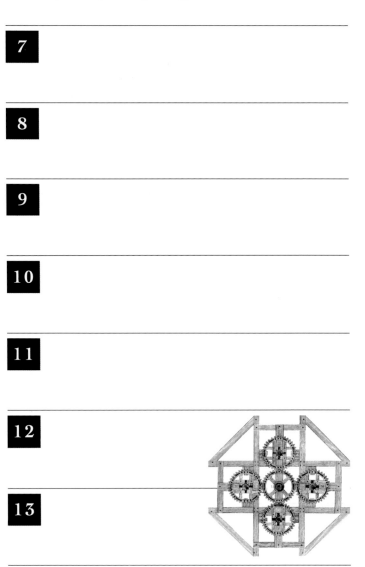

Top: A view of Moscow from the Kremlin. Bottom: The Bloody Massacre perpetrated in King Street... , *an engraving by Paul Revere depicting the Boston Massacre of March 5, 1770. This page: Machinery for boring cannon barrels from Gaspard Monge's* Description de l'art de fabriquer les canons, *Paris, 1790.*

c.1724 Gin becomes a popular drink in England. **1725** Excavations begin at Herculaneum. **1726** Jonathan Swift's *Gulliver's Travels* is published. **1727** Paper currency, backed by tobacco, is issued in Virginia. **1728** 5,000-volume Chinese encyclopedia, *Ku-chin t's-shu chi-ch'eng,* is published. **1729** Opium selling is prohibited in China by Emperor Yung Ch'eng. **1730** In American colonies, white stockings are fashionable for both men and women. **1732** Hermann Boerhaave's *Elements of Chemistry* is published forming the basis of organic chemistry. First American stagecoach route begins in New Jersey. **1732-43** Survey of Siberian coast by Russia. **1736** Leonard Euler publishes the first textbook of analytical mechanics. **1737** St. Patrick's Day is first celebrated in America by Protestants in support of unemployed Irish workers. **1741** Antonio Vivaldi composes *The Four Seasons.* **1742** The Swedish astronomer Anders Celsius introduces the centigrade thermometer. **1743** Handkerchiefs first manufactured in Scotland.

1700
to
1800

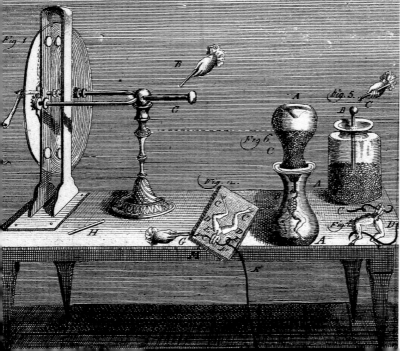

AUGUST

14

15

16

17

18

19

20

Top: Thomas Jefferson's rough draft of the Declaration of Independence, written in June 1776. Bottom left: In 1791, Luigi Galvani made public his findings about electricity. He mistakenly thought his experiments proved that animals themselves were the site of electricity. Right: Spanish playing cards, manufactured in France, c.1721-60.

1744 Rubber is first used in Europe. **1750** Population of Europe c.140 million. First volume of Diderot's *Encyclopedie* is published. **1751-52** Benjamin Franklin's *Experiments and Observations on Electricity* is published. **1753** Carlo Goldoni writes *La Locandiera*. **1755** Earthquake kills 30,000 in Lisbon. **1756-63** Seven Years' War (French and Indian War). **1757-74** Reign of Sultan Mustafa III in the Ottoman empire. **1757-89** Reign of Sidi Mohammed in Morocco. **1759** Franz Josef Haydn composes Symphony No. 1 in D Major. Columbia University is founded (as King's College). **1761** Electric harpsichord, the first electric instrument, is invented in Paris. **1762** Jean Jacques Rousseau writes *The Social Contract*. **1762-96** Reign of Catherine the Great in Russia. Six-year-old Wolfgang Amadeus Mozart tours Europe as a musical prodigy. **1764** Textile spinning is mechanized. **1765** The Stamp Act is passed by the British Parliament, requiring payment of tax on legal and commercial documents, newspapers and pamphlets in the American colonies.

صدقة السرطفي غضب الرب

قل رسول الله صلى الله عليه وسلم خيركم خيركم لاهله صدق رسول الله وقل خير التابعين وبس صدق رسول الله

1 7 0 0
to
1 8 0 0

A U G U S T

21

22

23

24

25

26

27

Top: A 1791 diploma for skill in Arabic calligraphy. The green sections contain statements from calligraphy masters attesting to the pupil's proficiency. Bottom left: Farming methods from the Encyclopedie, ou Dictionnaire raisonné des sciences, *Paris, 1762. Bottom right: Musicians rehearsing, from an engraving by George Balthasar Probst.*

1768 Sèvres is established as the state center for porcelain production in France. **1769** Scottish inventor James Watt patents a steam engine, ushering in the age of steam power. **1770** James Cook claims Australia for Great Britain. **c.1770** First modern circus ring is used for a performance. **1771** First edition of the *Encyclopædia Britannica* is published. **1773** Boston Tea Party. Oliver Goldsmith writes *She Stoops to Conquer.* The waltz is popular in Vienna. *Poems on Various Subjects, Religious and Moral* by Phillis Wheatley, the first black poet in the New World, is published in London. **1774** Louis XVI begins rule in France. Oxygen is isolated by Joseph Priestley. **1775-83** The American Revolution. **1776** Declaration of Independence is drafted by Thomas Jefferson. Adam Smith's *Inquiry Into the Nature and Causes of the Wealth of Nations,* treatise on political economy, is published. The first female suffrage law in the present U.S. is enacted in New Jersey; it is repealed in 1807. **1780** The *bolero* is introduced to Spain by Sebastian Cerezo.

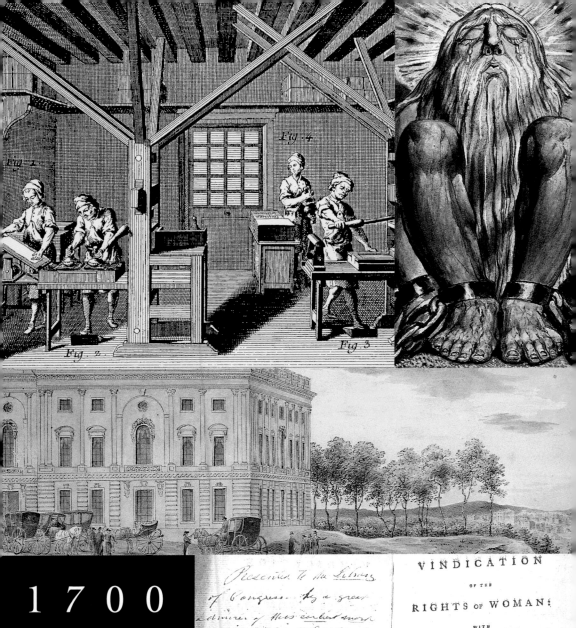

1700
to
1800

VINDICATION
OF THE
RIGHTS OF WOMAN:
WITH
STRICTURES
ON
POLITICAL AND MORAL SUBJECTS.

BY MARY WOLLSTONECRAFT.

AUGUST

28

29

30

31

1° SEPTEMBER

2

3

Top left: A French printing shop. Top right: From The Book of Urizen, *1794, by William Blake. Middle: The U.S. Capitol, unfinished in 1800, still was able to house Congress, the Supreme Court, and the Library of Congress. Bottom: A 1792 edition of* Vindication of the Rights of Woman. *This page: A Polish playing card for Trapola.*

c.1780 Tupac Amaru II leads an unsuccessful uprising of enslaved Indians against the Spanish in Upper Peru. **1781** Immanuel Kant writes *Critique of Pure Reason,* establishing his theory of rationalism of experience. **1785** First air crossing of the English Channel is made by Jean Pierre Blanchard and Dr. John Jeffries in a balloon. **1789** George Washington is inaugurated as the first president of the U.S. The French Revolution begins. Antoine Lavosier publishes his *Elementary Treatise on Chemistry.* **1791-92** Thomas Paine writes *The Rights of Man.* **1792** Denmark prohibits slave trade. Thomas Malthus' *Essay on the Principle of Population* is published. **1793** Eli Whitney invents the cotton gin (engine). **1794** The Qajar dynasty is founded in Iran. **1796** Napoleon marries Josephine. **1798** Edward Jenner creates a vaccine against smallpox. Aloys Senefelder invents lithography. **1799** The first modern configuration airplane is designed by Sir John Cayley. Pierre Laplace begins publishing treatise of knowledge on gravitational astronomy.

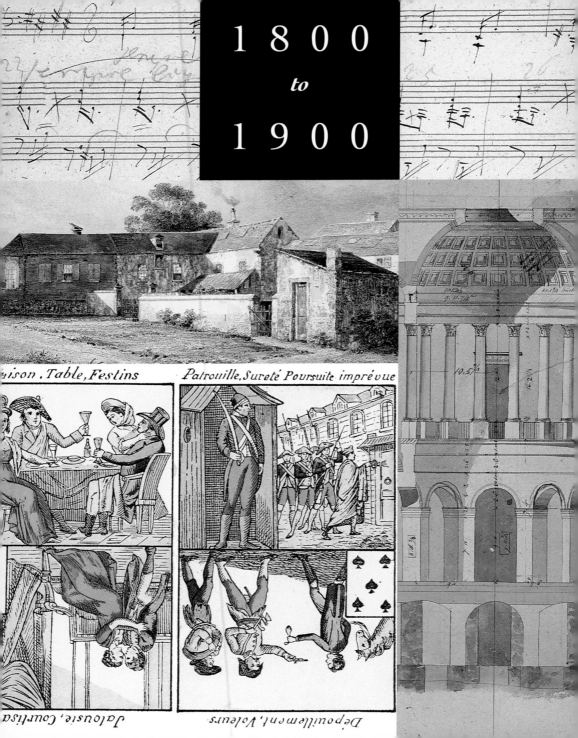

1800
to
1900

SEPTEMBER

4

5

6

7

8

9

10

Top: Beethoven's score of Sonata No. 30 in E Major, c.1820. Middle left: Longwood House, St. Helena Island, the site of Napoleon's death in 1821. Bottom left: French fortune-telling cards, c.1814-30. Right: The North Wing and Colonnade of the U.S. Capitol by Benjamin Latrobe, 1816. This page: A cannon, c.1850.

1800 Alessandro Volta invents the electric battery. Philadelphia is the only U.S. city with more than 50,000 inhabitants. **1801-25** Reign of Alexander I in Russia. **1803** United States doubles its size with the $15 million Louisiana Purchase from France. **1804** Napoleon proclaims himself emperor of France. The independent nation of Haiti is proclaimed (it is the second western hemisphere nation to gain independence, after the United States). **1806** Holy Roman Empire is abolished by Napoleon. **1807** Robert Fulton launches the *Clermont,* the first commercially successful steamship, on the Hudson River. **1808-14** The Peninsular War; France against Great Britain, Portugal, and Spanish guerrillas (Spain itself had a secret agreement to support France). **1809-10** Sir John Cayley publishes a treatise on aviation, laying groundwork for modern aerodynamics. **1810** Englishman Peter Durand patents the first tin can used for food storage. **1812** Napoleon's armies invade Russia in June; they retreat in winter, as most of the 600,000 men perish.

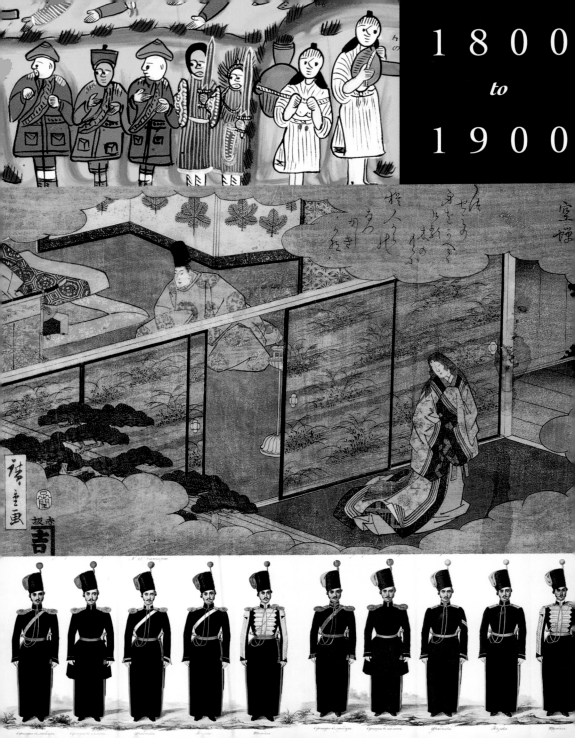

1800 to 1900

SEPTEMBER

11

12

13

14

15

16

17

Top: Ethiopian painting of the 1896 Battle of Aduwa during which the Ethiopians defeated invading Italians. Middle: An 1852 woodcut by Hiroshige of the Tale of Genji. *Bottom: Russian military uniforms of 1845. This page: "Costume for summer," a Sarony & Major lithograph, graces the sheet music cover of the 1851* Bloomer Waltz.

1814 Francisco Goya paints *Third of May, 1808,* as a denunciation of war. **1815** Napoleon is defeated by Wellington at Waterloo. **c.1815** Classical revival in architecture is prominent in Europe. **1816** Argentina declares independence from Spain. **1818** Chile declares independence from Spain. **1818-19** Théodore Géricault paints *The Raft of the "Medusa."* **1819** Philosopher Arthur Schopenhauer's *The World as Will and Representation* is published. **1820-22** Egyptian forces under Hussein conquer Sudan. **1821** Liberian capital of Monrovia (named for James Monroe) is founded as a haven for freed slaves. The harmonica is developed in Germany. **1822** Using the Rosetta Stone, Jean-François Champollion deciphers Egyptian hieroglyphics. Greece gains its independence from Turkey. **1823-43** Charles Babbage designs a calculating machine, a forerunner of the digital computer. **1824** Guadalupe Victoria is elected the first constitutional president of Mexico. **1825** First regular rail service begins in Great Britain.

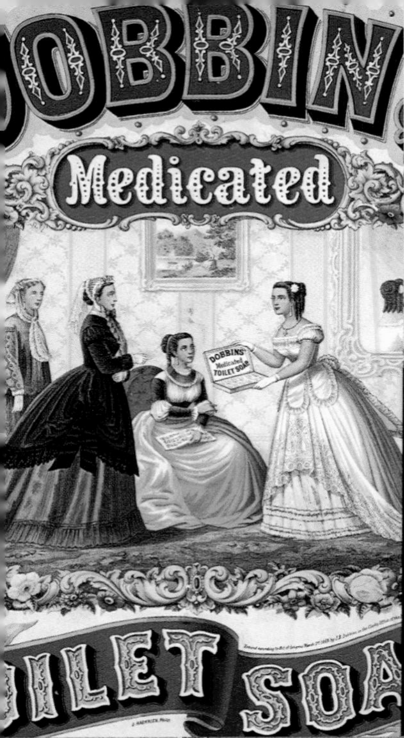

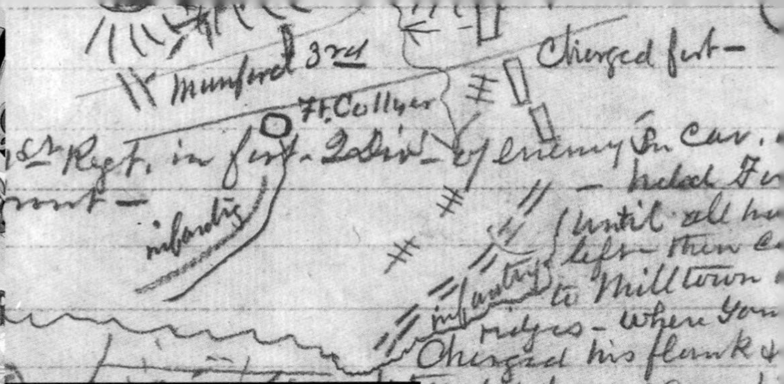

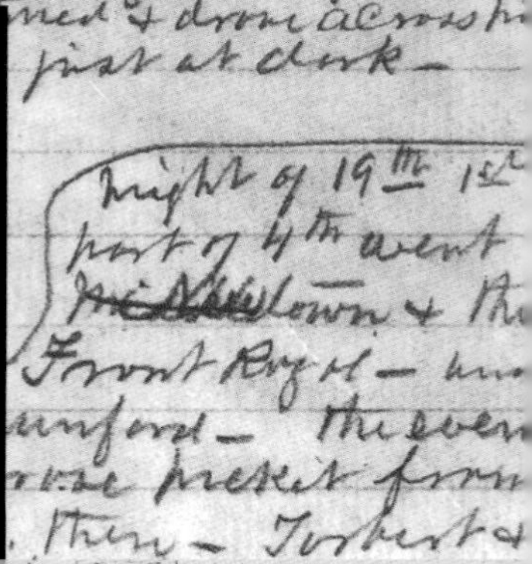

1800 *to* 1900

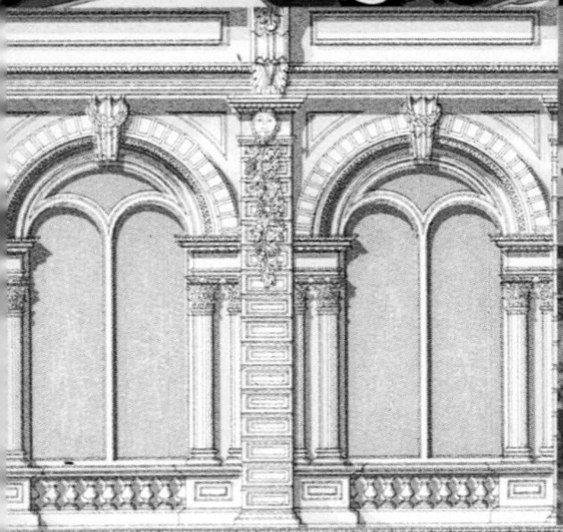

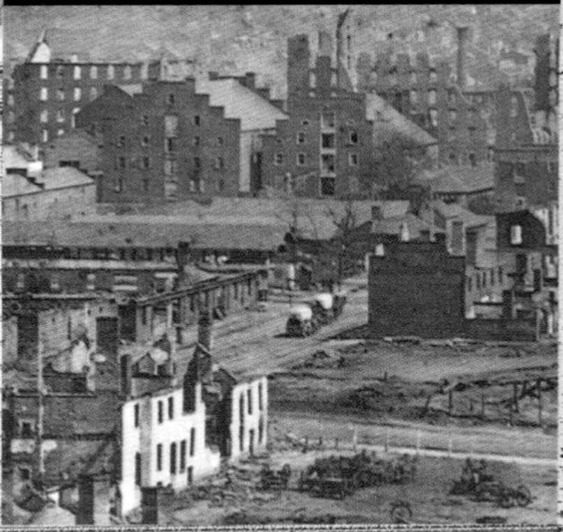

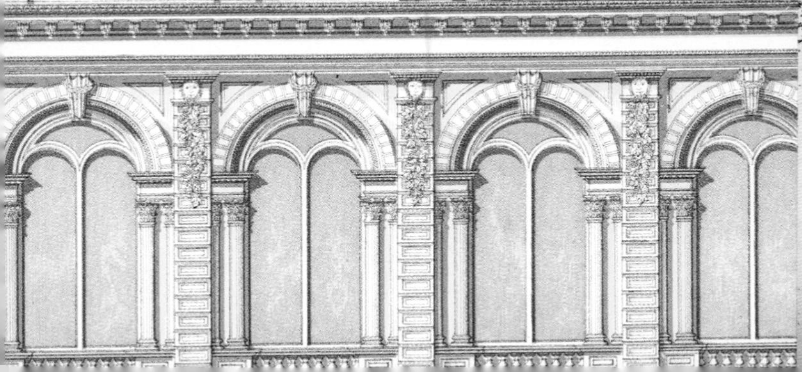

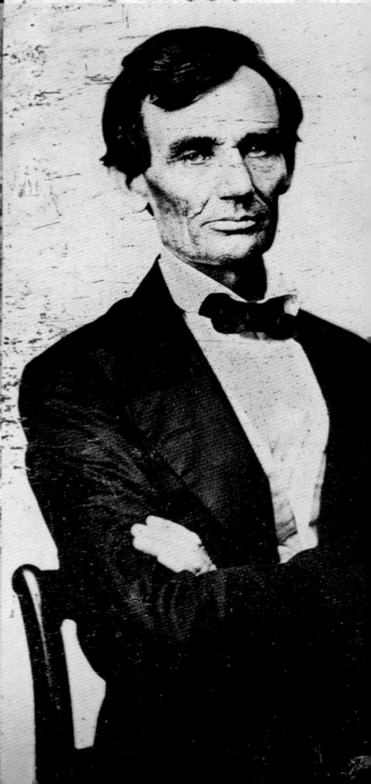

SEPTEMBER

18

19

20

21

22

23

24

Top left: Dobbins Medicated Toilet Soap ad, 1869. Top right: From the field notebook of Major Jedediah Hotchkiss, 1864. Bottom left: Cast-iron Banking House and Office building, 1865. Center: Alexander Gardner photo of Richmond, Virginia, April 1865. Bottom right: Ambrotype portrait of Abraham Lincoln, c.1855-60. This page: Walt Whitman.

1828 Friedrich Wohler synthesizes an organic compound (urea) from inorganic materials dispelling the notion of a "life force" in all organic compounds. **1830** Stendhal's *The Red and the Black* is published. **c.1830** Whole wheat Graham Crackers, named after health-food advocate the Reverend Sylvester Graham, originate in the U.S. **1837** Queen Victoria begins reign in England. Samuel Morse patents his model of the telegraph. **1838** Charles Dickens' *Oliver Twist* is published. **1838-53** Ieyoshi rules as shogun in Japan. **1839** Photography is first introduced to the public with the daguerreotype (invented by Louis Jacques Mande Daguerre). **1840** The first adhesive postage stamp, "penny black," goes on sale in England. **c.1840** Height of clipper ship era. **1842** The Boers found the Orange Free State in South Africa. **1843** Sören Kierkegaard's *Either/Or* is published. **1844** Chinese ports are opened to the United States. **1846** Elias Howe patents the sewing machine. Famine is widespread in Ireland as a result of the potato crop failure; 1 million die.

1 8 0 0

to

1 9 0 0

SEPTEMBER

25

26

27

28

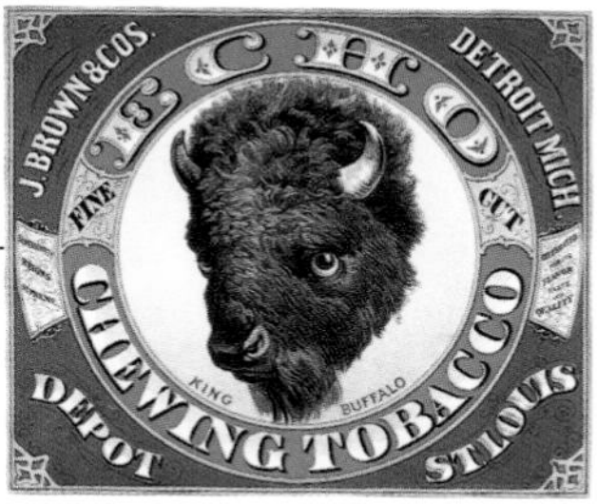

29

30

1 OCTOBER

Top left: Annie Oakley in 1899. Top right: A steamboat on the Mississippi in 1857. Bottom left: The game of lawn tennis in an L. Prang & Co. aquarelle. Right: "The Great Bartholdi Statue" (Statue of Liberty) in a Currier & Ives print of 1883, the year the statue was completed. This page: An 1873 ad for Echo Chewing Tobacco.

c.1846 First officially recorded modern baseball game played in Hoboken, New Jersey, between New York Nine and the Knickerbockers. **1847** James Joule publishes theory of conservation of energy. **1848** Revolutions throughout Europe against monarchies; the French Republic is formed. Karl Marx and Friedrich Engels publish the *Communist Manifesto*. Gold is discovered in California; San Francisco's population of 1,000 swells to 25,000 in two years. Lucretia Mott and Elizabeth Cady Stanton organize the first woman's rights convention at Seneca Falls, New York. **1850** Denim "Levi's" are first manufactured in San Francisco by Levi Strauss for miners. **c.1850** Height of the United States whaling industry. **1850-64** Popular uprising in China against the ruling Ch'ing dynasty. **1851** Rudolph Clausius states the second law of thermodynamics. Herman Melville's *Moby Dick* is published. **1852** Elisha G. Otis invents the elevator, leading (along with Bessemer's steel process) to the possibility of building skyscrapers.

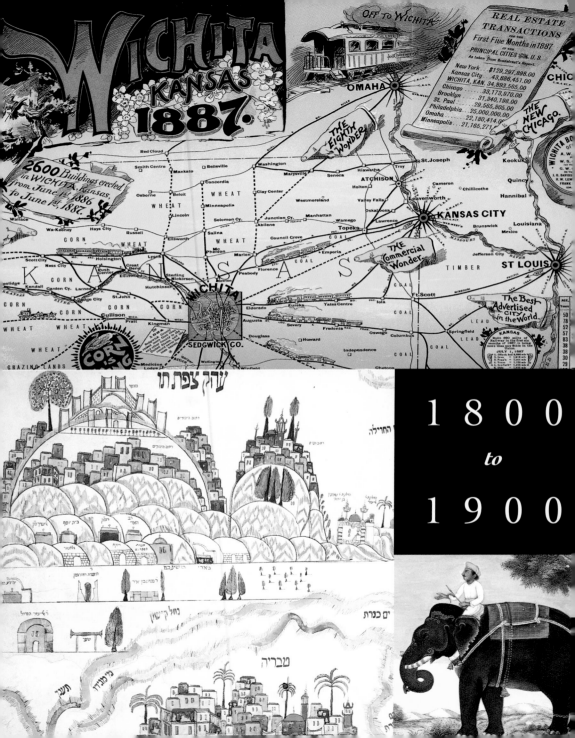

WICHITA KANSAS 1887.

OFF TO WICHITA

OMAHA

THE NEW CHICAGO.

REAL ESTATE TRANSACTIONS for the First Five Months in 1887 of the PRINCIPAL CITIES of the U.S. As taken from Bradstreet's Report.

New York	$129,297,898.00
Kansas City	43,686,451.00
WICHITA, KAN.	34,893,565.00
Chicago	33,173,970.00
Brooklyn	31,340,198.00
St. Paul	29,565,805.00
Philadelphia	25,000,000.00
Omaha	22,180,414.0
Minneapolis	21,165,271

2600 Buildings erected in WICHITA, Kansas, from June 1st, 1886 to June 1st, 1887.

THE EIGHTH WONDER

THE Commercial Wonder

The Best Advertised CITY in the World.

KANSAS CITY

ST LOUIS

KANSAS

CORN
WHEAT
COAL
TIMBER
LEAD
GRAZING LANDS

WICHITA SEDGWICK CO.

CORN'S G

1800 to 1900

זהר צפת

OCTOBER

2

3

4

5

6

7

8

Top: An 1887 railroad map shows all routes leading to Wichita, Kansas. Bottom left: Hebrew plaque from Palestine depicting shrines in Jerusalem, Safed, Tiberias, and Hebron. Bottom right: From the Persian manuscript Kitab-i tashrih al-aqvam. *This page: "Paris, New York & Philadelphia Fashions for Spring and Summer 1854."*

1853 Potato chips are developed in the town of Saratoga Springs, New York. Giuseppe Verdi composes *Il Trovatore* and *La Traviata.* **1854** Commodore Matthew Perry opens Japan to trade agreements with the U.S. **1856** Gustave Flaubert's *Madame Bovary* is published. **1858-66** Transatlantic cable is laid. **1859** Charles Darwin's *Origin of Species* is published. The French capture Saigon. **1860** Bessemer patents converter for turning iron into steel. **1860-61** Unification of Italy by Giuseppe Garibaldi. **1860-87** James Clerk Maxwell and Ludwig Boltzmann develop theory of statistical mechanics, accounting for bulk properties of all matter. **1861** U.S. Civil War begins. Telegraph line is laid across the U.S. Serfdom is abolished in Russia. **1863** French capture Mexico City; proclaim Archduke Maximilian of Austria emperor. Edouard Manet paints *Luncheon on the Grass.* **1864** Germ theory of disease is developed by Louis Pasteur. **1864-69** Leo Tolstoy writes *War and Peace.* **1865** United States President Abraham Lincoln is assassinated.

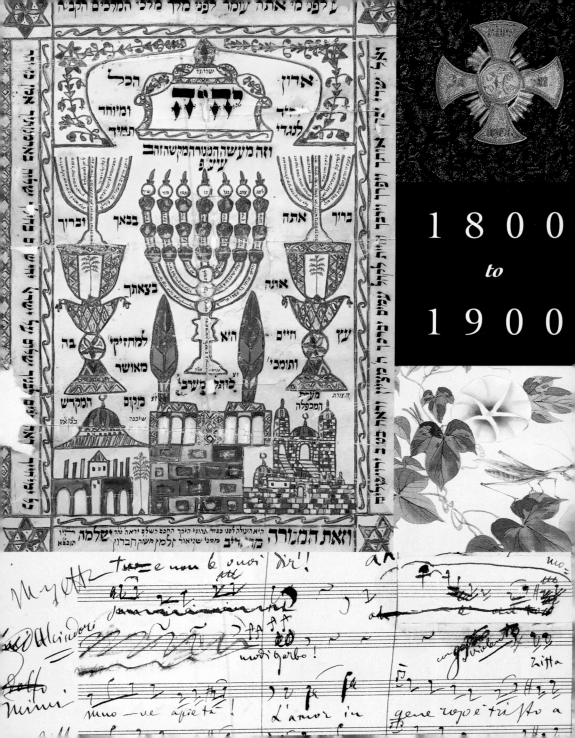

1800
to
1900

OCTOBER

9

10

11

12

13

14

15

Top left: The Jewish devotional Shiviti Plaque. Top right: Cover ornament of an 1899 Russian history of the czar's regiment. Center right: A Japanese painting on silk from an 1890 album of watercolors. Bottom: Giacomo Puccini's handwritten score of La Bohème, *1896. This page: The Maynard Rifle, 1860.*

c.1865 Lewis Carroll writes *Alice's Adventures in Wonderland.* Joseph Lister introduces antiseptic surgery practices. **1866** Fyodor Dostoyevsky writes *Crime and Punishment.* **1867** Alaska is purchased by U.S. from Russia for $7.2 million. Canada becomes a dominion. Dynamite is manufactured by Alfred Nobel. Japan ends 675-year rule by shoguns. **1867-94** Karl Marx writes *Das Kapital.* South African diamond fields open. **1869** U.S. population c.40 million. 100-mile-long Suez Canal is completed by French engineer Ferdinand de Lesseps. Campbell's soups are packaged in cans (they are "condensed" in 1898). The first U.S. transcontinental railroad is completed. Dmitri Mendeleev devises the periodic table of elements. **1871** Otto von Bismarck becomes chancellor of the German empire. P.T. Barnum opens his circus, "The Greatest Show on Earth," in New York City. The Chicago Fire destroys most of the city, which is made up of wooden buildings. **1872** Legendary ancient Troy is excavated by Hermann Schliemann.

1 8 0 0

to

1 9 0 0

Total Acres. Total Improved. Value Farm. Value Implements. Value Stock. Value Products.

OCTOBER

16	
17	
18	
19	
20	
21	
22	

Left: "Fred Ott's Sneeze," an 1893 motion picture. Top: X-ray by William Roentgen. Middle: Hermann Hollerith's 1894 punch card for his computing machine. Bottom right: This 1884 photograph of Oscar Wilde was the subject of a Supreme Court case to determine whether photography was an art and therefore protected under copyright law—it was.

1873 Work begins on a tunnel across the English Channel. Maxwell develops electrodynamic theory proposing that light is an electromagnetic wave. **1873-74** First Spanish Republic. **1875** Leo Tolstoy writes *Anna Karenina.* **1876** Alexander Graham Bell patents the telephone. Mark Twain writes *The Adventures of Tom Sawyer.* **1879** Thomas Edison invents the incandescent light bulb. **1880** Edgar Degas paints *Little Fourteen Year Old Dancer.* **1883** The Orient Express makes its inaugural run from Paris to Istanbul. The Brooklyn Bridge opens to great fanfare. Worldwide time zones are established with Greenwich mean time as the starting point. Friedrich Nietzsche's *Thus Spake Zarathustra* is published. **1884-93** The French claim protectorates and control large areas in Indochina. **1885** The modern internal combustion engine is developed by Gottlieb Daimler. **1886** Karl Benz patents a vehicle powered by a gasoline engine. Coca Cola formula is developed by a pharmacist in Atlanta, Georgia. **1888** Van Gogh paints *Sunflowers.*

THÉÂTRE NATIONAL DE L'OPÉRA-COMIQUE

CENDRILLON

CONTE de FÉES (d'après PERRAULT

PAR HENRI CAIN

MUSIQUE DE J. MASSENET

1 8 0 0

to

1 9 0 0

OCTOBER

23

24

25

26

27

28

29

FOR HEALTH & RECREATION
RIDE A CRAWFORD BICYCLE

$60 NONE BETTER FEW AS GOOD $75

Top left: An eleven-foot-wide poster for an 1856 circus touting "Five Celebrated Clowns." Bottom left: An 1899 poster for Massenet's Cendrillon *at the Opéra Comique, Paris. Right: Louis Sullivan's 1894 cast-iron Guaranty (Prudential) Building, Buffalo, New York. This page: An ad for Crawford Bicycles, c.1895.*

1888 George Eastman's Kodak camera ("anyone can use it") goes into production. Slavery is officially abolished in Brazil (last country to do so). **1889** Eiffel Tower is completed in Paris. **1893** New Zealand is the first nation to give the vote to women. Edvard Munch paints *The Scream.* **1894** Alfred Dreyfus is convicted of treason. Thomas Edison invents the Vitascope for motion pictures. **1894-95** Sino-Japanese War. **1895** X-rays are discovered by German physicist Wilhelm Roentgen. **1896** First modern Olympic Games are held in Athens, Greece. Giacomo Puccini writes *La Bohème.* **1897** China leases Hong Kong to Great Britain for 99 years. Greek and Turkish War. Karl Ferdinand Braun develops the cathode-ray tube. **1898** The Spanish American War begins as battleship *Maine* is blown up in Havana harbor. U.S. enters Cuban conflict; gains Puerto Rico, Guam, the Philippines, Hawaiian Islands. Radium is discovered by Marie and Pierre Curie. **1899** Scott Joplin's *Maple Leaf Rag* ushers in the ragtime craze in United States.

1 9 0 0

to

2 0 0 0

OCTOBER

30

31

1 NOVEMBER

FILMS DEVELOPED

By the Eastman developing
machine **While You Wait**

10 CENTS

Best Results   **No Scratches**

Eastman Kodaks and Supplies

FEAST & CO.

OPTICIANS   1213 F STREET

2

3

4

5

*Top: The Wright Brothers' historic flight at Kitty Hawk, North Carolina,
1903. Bottom left: 1900 Ivory Soap ad. Bottom middle: 1913 poster by G.K.
Benda of Parisian music hall singer Mistinguett. Bottom right: A cowboy
in a rare moment of leisure, photographed by Erwin E. Smith in 1905. This
page: Film developing ad in the 1905 playbill for* The Wizard of Oz.

1900 World population
c.1.5 billion. Max Planck
formulates the quantum
theory. Sigmund Freud
writes *Interpretation of
Dreams.* The escalator is
introduced at Paris Ex-
position. **1900-10** Eight
million immigrants arrive
in U.S. **1901** Russia completes the Trans-Siberian
railroad from Moscow to
Port Arthur. Adrenalin is
isolated. First Nobel Prizes
are awarded.**1902** Aswan
Dam is completed. **1903**
The first powered, con-
trolled airplane flight in
history is made by Orville
and Wilbur Wright at
Kitty Hawk, North Car-
olina. The first movie with
a complete plot, the ten-
minute *The Great Train
Robbery,* is produced. The
electrocardiograph is in-
vented. **1904** The Russo-
Japanese War begins.
1905 First Russian Revolution. Albert Einstein
announces special theory
of relativity, introducing
$E=mc^2$. Rayon is first commercially manufactured.
1906 San Francisco earthquake.**1907** The word
"television" is first used.
1908 Henry Ford mass
produces the Model T,
which sells for $850. **1908-
12** Reign of Hsuan-t'ung,
the last emperor of China.

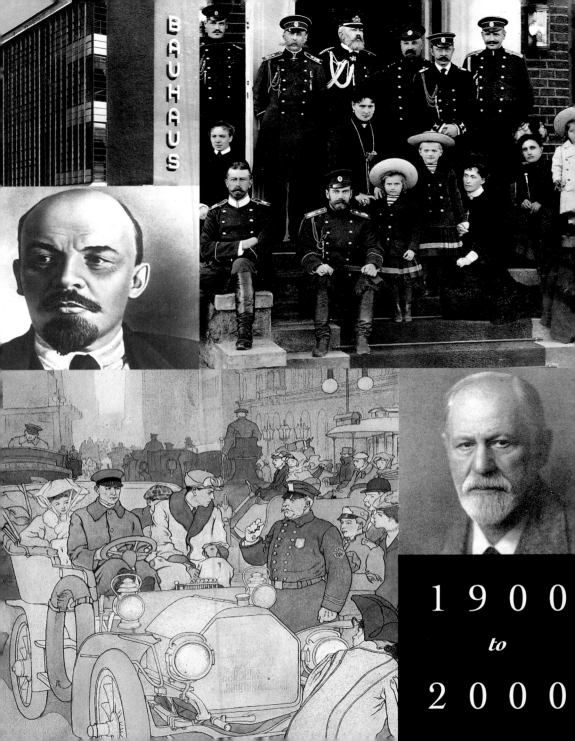

BAUHAUS

1900

to

2000

NOVEMBER

6

7

8

9

10

11

12

Top left: Bauhaus, Dessau, Germany, 1925, designed by Walter Gropius, who formed the "guild of craftsmen, free of class-dividing arrogance...." Top right: Czar Nicholas II and family, c.1900. Left middle: Vladimir Il'ich Lenin, 1920. Bottom left: Edward Penfield's cover of Collier's *magazine, 1907. Right: Sigmund Freud, c.1915. This page: Study chair; 1917.*

1909 Armenians revolt against Ottoman rule. Bakelite is manufactured commercially. **1910** Stravinsky's *The Firebird* is performed in Paris by the Ballets Russes. **1911** Chinese Revolution; the Ch'ing dynasty is overthrown. Roald Admussen reaches the South Pole. **1912** *Pravda* is first published in St. Petersburg; Josef Stalin is an editor. Delhi becomes the capital of India. C.G. Jung's *Theory of Psychoanalysis* is published. **1913** D.H. Lawrence writes *Sons and Lovers*. **1913-27** Marcel Proust writes *Remembrance of Things Past*. **1914** The Panama Canal is completed. The first red and green traffic lights are used in Cleveland, Ohio. **1914-18** World War I; begins with assassination of Archduke Franz-Ferdinand at Sarajevo. **1914-21** James Joyce writes *Ulysses*. **1915** Gregori Rasputin's influence predominates in Russia. D.W. Griffith's film *Birth of a Nation* is released. The speed record for automobiles is 102.6 mph. **1917** U.S. enters World War I. The Russian Revolution; Bolsheviks institute the first Communist national government.

VOTES FOR US
- WHEN -
WE ARE WOMEN

US

OMEN

NOVEMBER

13

14

15

16

17

18

19

LES BALLETS RUSSES
COMŒDIA ILLUSTRE

MAISON
RUSSE   1910   OPERA
BALLETS

Top: Frank Lloyd Wright's Emil Bach House, Chicago, 1915. Bottom left: A 1913 demonstration in favor of women's suffrage. Right: Fashionable outfits in McCall's *magazine, 1910. This page: Program cover for the 1910 season of the Ballets Russes during which the premiere of Stravinsky's* The Firebird *was performed.*

1917 Sigmund Freud's *Introduction to Psychoanalysis* is published. **1918** Serbo-Croat-Slovene kingdom of Yugoslavia formed. Worldwide flu epidemic kills c.25 million. **1919** First international air mail service is introduced between Paris and London. League of Nations is formed. **1920** Nineteenth Amendment, extending vote to women in U.S., is ratified. Population of New York City is 5.6 million. The "Tommy" (submachine) gun, is patented by John T. Thompson, for whom it is named. **1921** Kingdom of Iraq is created from the former Mesopotamia. **1922** Mussolini marches on Rome; forms fascist government. Insulin is first given to diabetics. **1923** Pancho Villa, Mexican rebel leader, is assassinated in Mexico. First non-stop transcontinental flight from New York to San Diego in 26 hours, 50 minutes. The electric razor is patented. **1924** Greece becomes a republic. Thomas Mann's *The Magic Mountain* is published. **1925** Reza Khan becomes shah of Persia, beginning Pahlavi dynasty. Adolf Hitler publishes *Mein Kampf*, vol. 1.

1 9 0 0

to

2 0 0 0

NOVEMBER

20

21

22

23

24

25

26

Top: The Dionne Quintuplets, the world's most famous babies c.1935. Left: New York Yankee Babe Ruth, 1920. Middle: Charlie Chaplin in The Kid, *which also featured Jackie Coogan, 1921. Right: Charles Lindbergh after his historic flight, May 21, 1927. This page: Poster for the classic film* Casablanca, *1942.*

1925 Dmitri Shostakovich composes his Symphony No. 1. The Charleston, a popular dance, becomes a symbol of the Roaring Twenties. Nellie Taylor Ross, the first U.S. woman governor, is elected in Wyoming. **1926** T.E. Lawrence writes *The Seven Pillars of Wisdom.* Nationalist China is united by General Chiang Kai-shek. **1927** In the single-engine *Spirit of St. Louis* Charles A. Lindbergh completes the world's first solo nonstop transatlantic flight. *The Jazz Singer,* the first talking movie, is released. New York Yankee Babe Ruth hits a record 60 home runs. **1928** D.H. Lawrence writes *Lady Chatterly's Lover.* Penicillin is discovered by Alexander Fleming. **1929** Leon Trotsky is expelled from the U.S.S.R. Crash of the New York Stock Exchange leads to the Great Depression. First Academy Awards take place. Clarence Birdseye introduces frozen foods. **1930** Gandhi leads protest march against Indian government's salt tax. Constantinople's name is changed to Istanbul. Ras Tafari becomes Haile Selassie of Ethiopia.

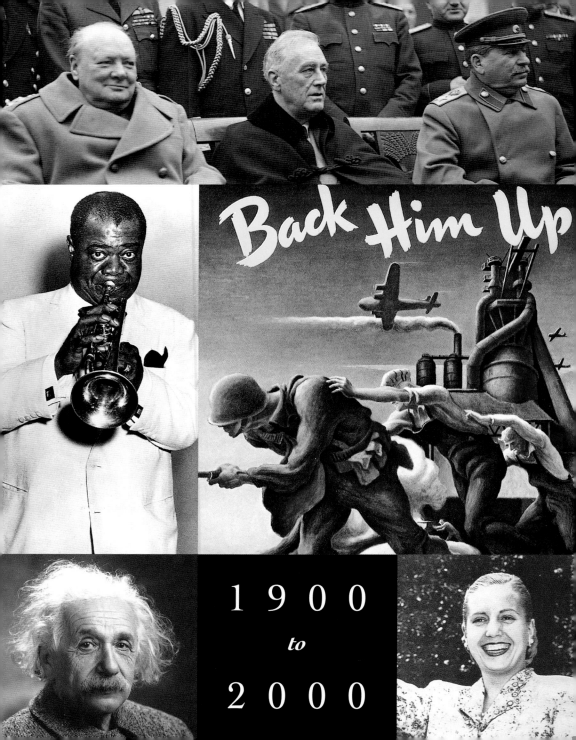

Back Him Up

1900
to
2000

NOVEMBER

27	
28	
29	
30	
1	DECEMBER
2	
3	

Top: Winston Churchill, F.D. Roosevelt, Josef Stalin at the Yalta Conference, 1945. Middle left: Louis ("Satchmo") Armstrong, 1964. Middle right: World War II poster by Thomas Hart Benton. Bottom left: Albert Einstein, 1947. Bottom right: Eva Perón, wife of Argentine President Juan Perón. This page: Suzy Perette's "Bubble" skirt, 1957.

c.1930 U.S. population 123 million. One in five Americans owns a car. **1931** Salvador Dali paints *The Persistence of Memory*. Process for manufacture of synthetic rubber is devised. Empire State Building, world's tallest, is completed. **1932** Franklin D. Roosevelt is elected president of U.S. Aldous Huxley writes *Brave New World*. Amelia Earhart is first woman to fly solo across Atlantic. **1933** Roosevelt proclaims the New Deal. Hitler is appointed German chancellor. Federico Garcia Lorca writes *The Blood Wedding*. U.S. goes off the gold standard. **1934** Stalin begins bloody purge of opponents in party. **1934-35** Radar is developed. **1936** Spanish Civil War begins. Jesse Owens wins four gold medals at the Berlin Olympics. **1937** Second Sino-Japanese War. **1939** Poland invaded by Germany. **1939-45** World War II. **1940** Nylon stockings are first available for sale. Xerography process is patented. **1941** German armies invade Russia. Japan attacks Pearl Harbor, bringing U.S. into war. **1942** Enrico Fermi produces first nuclear chain reaction.

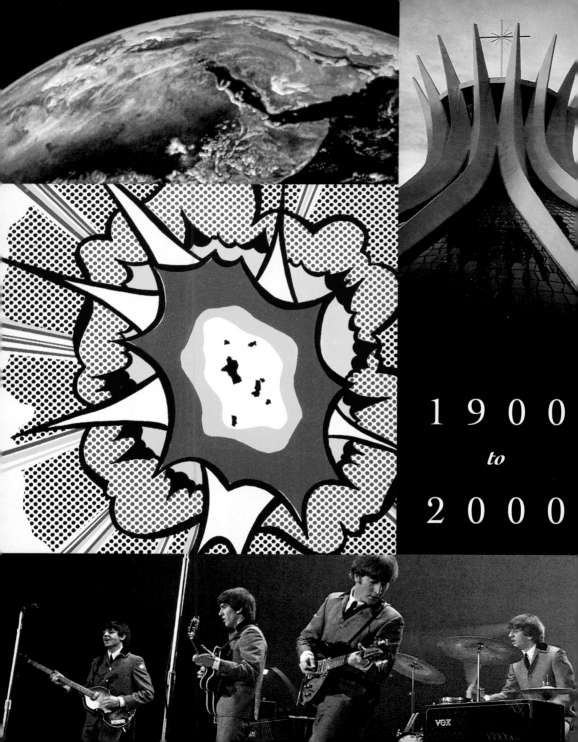

1 9 0 0

to

2 0 0 0

DECEMBER

4

5

6

7

The New York Times

"All the News That's Fit to Print"

LATE CITY EDITION

VOL. CXVIII. No. 40,721   NEW YORK, MONDAY, JULY 21, 1969   10 CENTS

MEN WALK ON MOON

8

9

10

Top left: Earth as seen from space. Top right: The cathedral at Brasilia, a city built in the jungles of Brazil, planned as the new capital. Center: Detail of Roy Lichtenstein's Pop Art painting, Explosion, *1967. Bottom: The Beatles in concert, February 1964. This page:* New York Times *front page, July 21, 1969, announcing man's first moon landing.*

1945 World's first atom bomb is dropped on Hiroshima, Japan. First regularly scheduled transatlantic passenger airline service begins. **1946** Winston Churchill uses phrase "Iron Curtain" in a speech. **1947** Charles Yaeger is first pilot to exceed the speed of sound. India becomes independent; Pakistan is formed. **1948** Israel becomes a nation. The term "Cold War" is coined by statesman Bernard Baruch. Gandhi is assassinated in New Delhi. **1949** Indian law abolishes "untouchable" class. Communists are victorious in Chinese Civil War; Communist People's Republic of China is formed. NATO is founded. Simone de Beauvoir writes *The Second Sex.* **1950** U.S. population 150 million. **1950-53** The Korean War. **1953** Stalin dies. Francis H.C. Crick and James D. Watson propose double-helix structure for DNA, a breakthrough in genetics. A. Scott Crossfield is the first pilot to fly at twice the speed of sound (Mach 2). **1954** The Algerian War of Independence against France begins. (France agrees to Algeria's independence in 1962).

1900
to
2000

DECEMBER

11

12

13

14

15

16

17

Left: An array of TV sets in a 1970 showroom; a year earlier 600 million viewed the first landing of humans on the moon on TV. Right top: Martin Luther King, Jr., 1965. Middle: Mao Tse-tung. Middle below: Fidel Castro. Bottom left: Malcolm X. Right: Indira Gandhi. This page: A 1967 Soviet poster celebrates fifty years of Communism.

1955 Rosa Parks is arrested for refusing to move from the "whites only" section of a bus in Montgomery, Alabama, triggering boycotts leading to U.S. Civil Rights movement. The Warsaw Pact is formed. **1956** Egypt takes control of the Suez Canal. Elvis Presley appears on *The Ed Sullivan Show,* introducing Rock 'n' Roll to millions. **1957** *Sputnik 1,* the first man-made earth-orbit satellite, is launched by Soviets; the Space Age begins. Ghana gains independence. **1959** Cuban President Fulgencio Batista flees; Fidel Castro takes over. **1960** First laser is built. John F. Kennedy, age 43, becomes youngest elected U.S. president. "Sit-ins" begin in U.S. southern states to protest lunch counter segregation. **1961** East Germans erect the Berlin Wall. Russian Yuri Gagarin becomes the first man in space, in a one-orbit mission on *Vostok.* **1962** Cuban missile crisis. **1963** John F. Kennedy is assassinated in Dallas. Betty Friedan writes *The Feminine Mystique.* Valentina Tereshkova is the first woman in space, aboard *Vostok 6.*

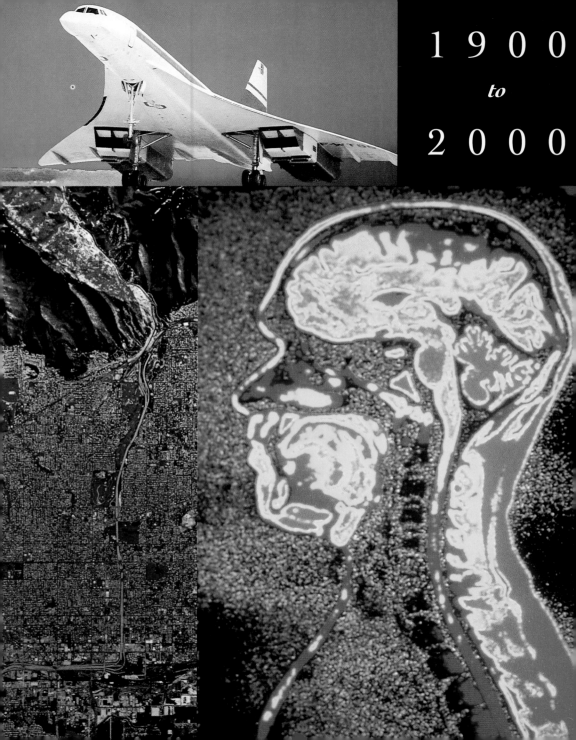

1 9 0 0
to
2 0 0 0

DECEMBER

18

19

20

21

22

23

24

Top: The Concorde SST, the only commercial jetliner that flies faster than the speed of sound. Left: A Landsat photo of Salt Lake City taken from space. Right: MRI (magnetic resonance image) of the human body, used for medical diagnosis. This page: Ubiquitous CDs (compact disks), which deliver digital information, have changed entertainment and business.

1965 First commercial non-stop Pacific Ocean crossing by air in 14 hours, 33 minutes, from San Francisco to Sydney. Alexi Leonov is the first person to "walk in space." Malcolm X is assassinated. **1966** U.S. has c.190,000 troops in South Vietnam. **1966-68** Race riots in American cities. **1966-76** Cultural Revolution in China. **1967** Cuban guerilla leader Che Guevara is killed in Bolivia. Israel victorious in the Six Day War against Egypt, Syria, Jordan, Lebanon, and Iraq. **1968** Martin Luther King, Jr., is slain in Memphis. Robert F. Kennedy is assassinated in Los Angeles. TV sets are in 98 percent of U.S. homes. **1969** "The Eagle has landed": Neil A. Armstrong, Edwin E. Aldrin, Jr., are first humans to land on moon as 600 million watch on TV. **1971-79** Idi Amin in power in Uganda. **1972** U.S. President Richard Nixon visits Communist China. CAT scans are introduced for medical diagnosis. **1973** Salvador Gossens Allende, Chilean president, is killed in overthrow of his regime. **1975** Last American soldiers to officially leave Vietnam.

1900 to 2000

DECEMBER

25

26

27

28

29

30

31

Left: The double-helix DNA structure in a computer model. Right: The Ginza district of Tokyo. Bottom: A silicon computer-chip circuit board, with its ability to compress digital data, is the basis for the information revolution. This page: A "mouse" that is sometimes used instead of a keyboard to move the cursor on a computer display.

1976 *Viking II* lands on Mars. **1978** Personal computers are available for consumers. **1979** Islamic Republic proclaimed by Ayatollah Khomeni in Iran. **1980** Strikes in Poland by the labor union Solidarity. **1981** AIDS virus is identified. MTV goes on the air. Facsimile (fax) machines come into use. **1982** First artificial heart transplant in a human. **1984** Novelist William Gibson first uses the word "cyberspace." **1985** Mikhail Gorbachev comes to power in Soviet Union. **1988** Parallel computers are developed. **1989** Berlin Wall is dismantled; Communism falls in eastern Europe. Space probe *Voyager* travels 2.8 million miles to limits of the solar system. **1990** Germany is reunified. Akihito, son of Hirohito, is proclaimed 125th successor to throne of Japan. Playwright Vaclev Havel is elected president of Czechoslovakia. **1993** Apartheid ends in South Africa. **1995** Millions of people in 160 countries are connected by the global Internet. In the U.S. there are PCs for one in every four people. **2000** World population c.6.5 billion.

Acknowledgments

We would like to thank the following individuals at the Library of Congress, especially then-Director of Publishing Dana Pratt for his early enthusiasm for our project. The Publishing Office acted as the Library's coordinating point for this book. Margaret Wagner was an incomparable resource and our strong supporter even as deadline pressures mounted. Thanks must also go to John Y. Cole, Acting Director of Publishing, to Susan Sharp and Sara Day, and to picture researcher Corinne Szabo for providing last-minute assistance in tracking images for a wide range of dates and events.

Visual materials in this volume were drawn from many areas of the Library including: the General Collections, the Rare Book and Special Collections Division (with special thanks to Dr. Joan Higbee), the Prints and Photographs Division, the Geography and Map Division, the Music Division, the Asian Division, the Motion Picture, Broadcasting and Recorded Sound Division, and the Manuscript Division.

In New York, Marijke Smit provided research assistance and fact checking for the timeline.

The book is immeasurably better for all of their help.

E.P. and J.H.
New York, 1995